Floppy's Phonics

Sounds and Letters

# Teaching Handbook 1

## Contents



## Photocopiable resources:




**Written by Debbie Hepplewhite**

**Series created by Roderick Hunt and Alex Brychta**

OXFORD
UNIVERSITY PRESS

Great Clarendon Street, Oxford, OX2 6DP, United Kingdom

Oxford University Press is a department of the University of Oxford. It furthers the University's objective of excellence in research, scholarship, and education by publishing worldwide.



First published 2011

This edition published by Oxford University Press 2011



ISBN: 978-0-19-848603-9

7 9 10 8

Printed in Great Britain by Ashford Colour Press

Paper used in the production of this book is a natural, recyclable product made from wood grown in sustainable forests. The manufacturing process conforms to the environmental regulations of the country of origin.

**Acknowledgements:**
The publisher would like to thank the following for permission to reproduce artwork:
**p21** Geom/Shutterstock; **p27** Daniel Gale/Shutterstock; **p30, p33** Suzie Williams OUP; **p36** Monkey Business Images/Shutterstock

Page make-up and illustrations on p69-112 by Oxford Designers and Illustrators

Dear Colleague,

Welcome to the *Oxford Reading Tree Floppy's Phonics Sounds and Letters* programme!

Throughout my years as a teacher and head teacher, I wanted to find a better way of ensuring that *every child* in the school learned to read and spell well. I read widely about the research on reading and began to advise and train on the principles of teaching synthetic phonics.

I've now teamed up with Oxford University Press to develop a comprehensive set of phonics resources to provide teachers with everything they need to teach children the alphabetic code. This will enable children to read, spell and write well no matter what their individual needs and abilities are.

*Oxford Reading Tree Floppy's Phonics Sounds and Letters* is a rigorous and systematic synthetic phonics programme, which offers comprehensive multi-sensory resources and practical guidance to support teaching and learning in school and at home.

The resources are fully integrated with the rest of *Oxford Reading Tree* to enable you to continue to use the materials you already know. I feel honoured and thrilled to be invited to help with creating such a thorough synthetic phonics programme building on the delightful, well-known characters, storylines and illustrations of Biff, Chip and Kipper!

I hope you enjoy the programme. I will be running training sessions to support you and your school in implementing synthetic phonics and to offer advice. I hope to see you there!

Good luck and best wishes,

Debbie Hepplewhite

# What is Floppy's Phonics Sounds and Letters?

*Floppy's Phonics Sounds and Letters* is a rigorous, systematic synthetic phonics programme that offers highly practical guidance and comprehensive multi-sensory resources to support teaching and learning in school and at home.

The resources of the *Floppy's Phonics Sounds and Letters* programme are integrated with a range of decodable *Floppy's Phonics Fiction* and *Non-fiction* books for reading practice.

## The Sounds and Letters Teaching Sequence

### 1. Revisit and Review

- Revise sounds and graphemes using the *Flashcards* and *Frieze*.

### 2. Teach

- Teach the new sound and grapheme using the *Flashcards* and the *Sounds and Letters* CD-ROM.

### 3. Practise

- Practise new and revised sounds and graphemes with the *Sounds and Letters Books* and the Activity Sheets.

## 4. Apply

After each new sound and grapheme:

- Use the Cumulative Texts for reading practice.
- Use the Grapheme Tiles for spelling practice.

## 5. Consolidate

After each set of 3 or 4 sounds and graphemes:

- Use the *Sounds and Letters Books* for revision and to build confidence. Activities at the end of each book consolidate learning.
- Encourage individual use of the *Sounds and Letters* CD-ROM activities.

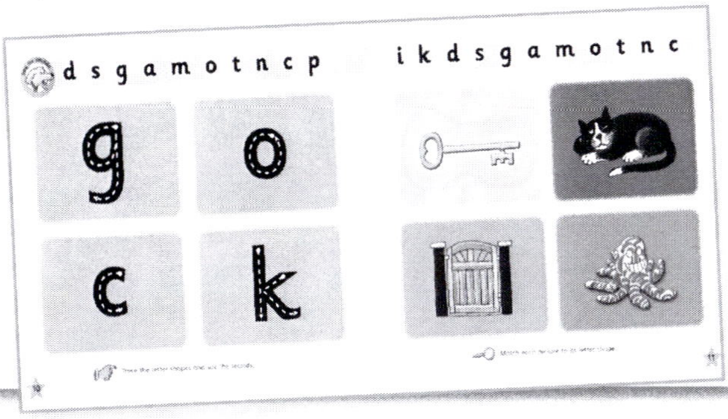

## 6. Further Practise

After each stage of the *Sounds and Letters Books*:

- Practise reading stories with *Floppy's Phonics Fiction*.
- Practise reading different text types with *Floppy's Phonics Non-fiction*.

**100%** matched to the Letters and Sounds phases

# A closer look at the resources

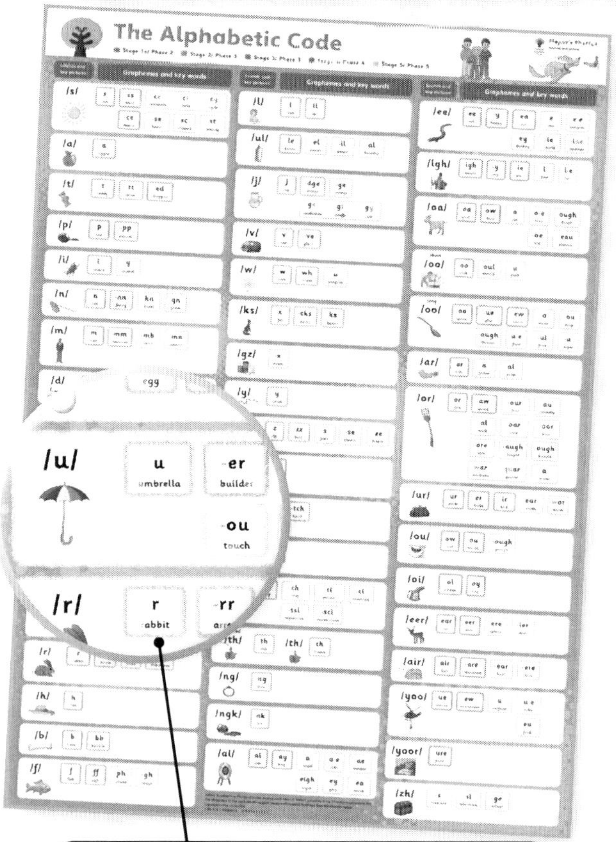


The graphemes are colour-coded according to the *Oxford Reading Tree* stage at which they are introduced.

## The Alphabetic Code Chart

At the heart of the programme is the *Alphabetic Code Chart*.

This chart shows the relationship between 50 units of sound (including 43 phonemes) and the graphemes which represent these sounds. It displays the sounds with key pictures, followed by alternative spellings (graphemes) of these sounds and key word examples.

It should be displayed to:

- help children remember how to understand the alphabetic code
- help parents understand the code and how phonics is being taught
- provide a permanent reference chart to support both planned and incidental phonics teaching.

There is a quick reference version of this chart in the *Planning, Assessment and Resources* book (pages 31–32), and some supporting notes on pages 14–19 of this handbook.

## The Alphabet Poster

The *Alphabet Poster* shows both lower case and capital letters on writing lines in alphabetical order to support the correct writing of letter shapes. Starting dots, dashes and arrows indicate directionality.

## The Tricky Words Poster

The Tricky Words Poster draws attention to words which are common but may have tricky parts. Words are grouped in families such as 'to, do, into' and 'no, so, go, oh no!'. It includes the *Letters and Sounds* high frequency word list for Phases 2 to 5.

## The Frieze

Use the *Frieze* to revise sounds and graphemes. The *Frieze* shows the focus graphemes along with key mnemonic pictures and words. Each strip matches one *Sounds and Letters Book*, so the *Frieze* can be displayed on the wall as the children learn each set of sounds.

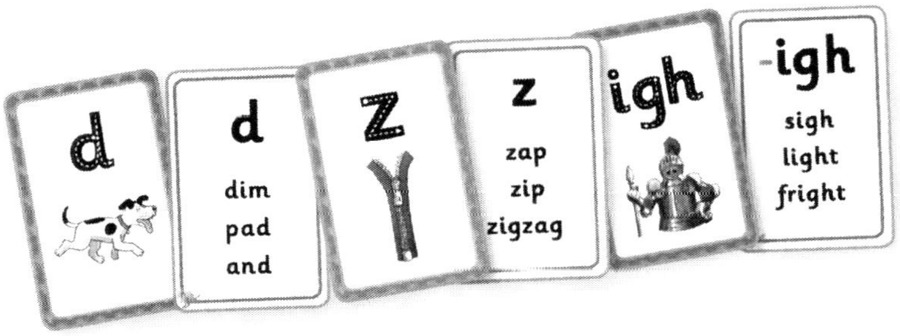


## The Flashcards

There are 72 A4 *Flashcards* to teach new sounds and graphemes. On the front they show the key mnemonic pictures which appear throughout the resources. On the back there is a list of carefully selected words which can be used to model blending and segmenting.

## Interactive Whiteboard CD-ROM

Teach the new sounds and graphemes using the interactive *Sounds and Letters* CD-ROM.

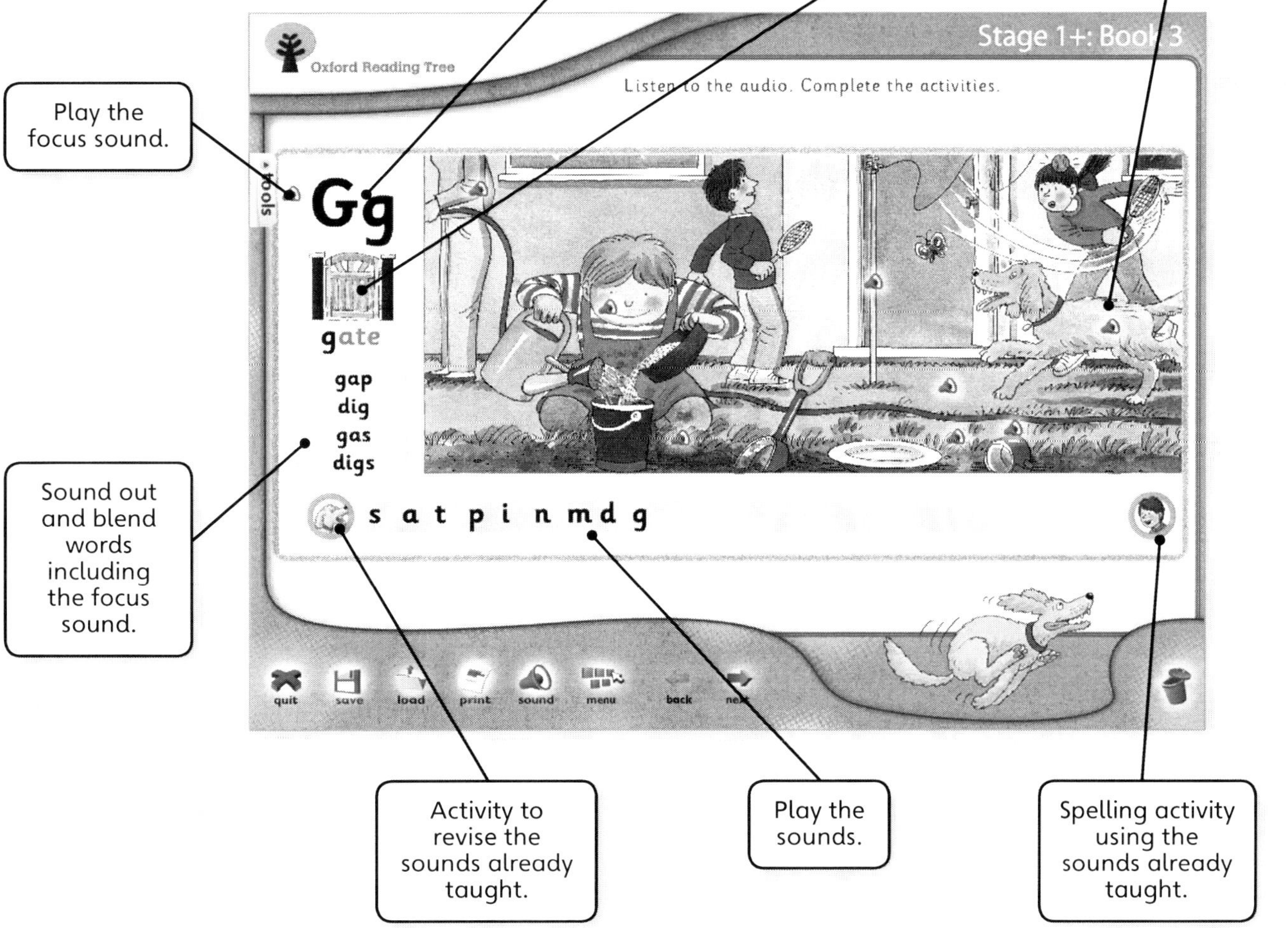

## Sounds and Letters Books

There are 42 *Sounds and Letters Books* at Stages 1 to 5 (*Letters and Sounds* Phases 1 to 5). They practise sounds and graphemes in the context of *Oxford Reading Tree* scenes. You can find the programme structure chart on page 20 of this handbook.

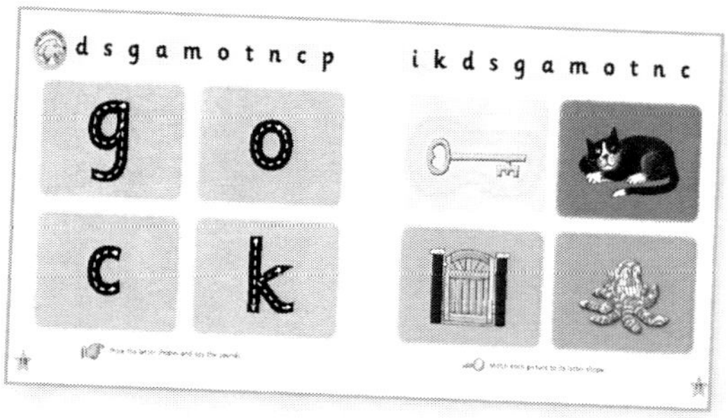


Each book introduces and practises 3 or 4 sounds and provides consolidation activities including matching activities, captions, texts and short stories at the end of each book. There is also support for parents and teaching assistants on the inside covers of every book.

### Stage 1

These six rich picture books feature Biff, Chip and Kipper and focus on environmental sounds in different settings, such as at the farm, at the park and at school.

Rich illustrations to explore together.

Key sounds in the scene are highlighted in the focus panel.

Questions and prompts to help adult and child to make the most of the book.

### Stages 1+ to 3

List of decodable words to read which include the focus grapheme.

Capital and lower case traceable letters.

Key word and picture.

Labels to show the focus sound and grapheme in context. Hints to help children find as many things in the picture featuring the focus sound.

'Say the sounds' bar to practise all of the sounds as quickly as possible.

## Activity Sheets

There is one photocopiable Activity Sheet for every grapheme introduced: 60 in *Handbook 1* (Stages 1+, 2 and 3) and 74 in *Handbook 2* (Stages 4 and 5).

Children can practise their reading and writing skills through activities such as letter-tracing, saying the sound and key word, blending to read words, writing the grapheme, orally segmenting words and gradually progressing to reading and writing simple sentences. The Activity Sheets are ideal for use in the classroom and for sending home to revise learning and inform parents.

## Teaching Handbooks

The *Teaching Handbooks* are straightforward guides to the programme packed with photocopiable resources.

They include:

- step-by-step guidance for each phonics session
- a bank of additional activities for each stage of *Floppy's Phonics Sounds and Letters*
- Photocopiable resources:
  - Activity Sheets for phonics practice
  - Say the Sounds Posters – these can be used to say the sounds and point to the graphemes (when the adult says the sounds), for a visual writing prompt, for ongoing self-assessment and periodic formal assessment.

## Planning, Assessment and Resources Book and CD-ROM

The *Planning, Assessment and Resources Book* and CD-ROM offers guidance and resources to help manage teaching and assessment. It includes:

- Planning grids
- Assessment sheets
- Cumulative Texts: for every sound and grapheme introduced, there are two short, unseen cumulative texts (without picture cues) for reading practice, spelling practice and assessment.
- Grapheme Tiles: these are small paper-based tiles which can be used flexibly in various adult-led activities and pupil activities both at school and at home.

The CD-ROM contains lesson plans which can be edited and customised to suit your needs.

# The new Oxford Reading Tree

*Oxford Reading Tree* is a much-loved and comprehensive reading programme that has taught millions of children to read. The loveable characters accompany children every step of the way from learning phonics to enjoying the rich *Biff, Chip and Kipper Stories*. Big helpings of fun, magic and drama all help to inspire a real love of reading.

Each *Oxford Reading Tree* stage includes a breadth of reading with progression in small gradual steps to help every child progress. The books are book-banded and matched to *Letters and Sounds* making them easy to manage, even in the busiest of classrooms.

The *Floppy's Phonics Sounds and Letters* programme has been created to teach children the alphabetic code and the reading skills they need to enjoy as many stories as possible!

**Teach Phonics**
**with Floppy's Phonics Sounds and Letters**
All you need to deliver *Letters and Sounds* and more!

→

**Practise Phonics**
**with Floppy's Phonics Fiction and Non-fiction**
Fully decodable books to build reading confidence!

→

**Richer Reading**
**with 36 new Biff, Chip and Kipper Decode and Develop Stories**
Plus 228 other fantastic Biff, Chip & Kipper Stories.

## The characters

The *Oxford Reading Tree* characters, Biff, Chip, Kipper and Floppy, were created 25 years ago, but they are still as popular as ever! In a poll by Booktrust, Biff, Chip and Kipper were voted children's fourth favourite literary characters beating well known characters such as Doctor Who, Alex Rider, Thomas the Tank Engine and Winnie The Pooh (*The Guardian*, 20 October 2009).

### The Robinson family

Dad

Mum

*Biff and Chip are twins.*

Biff

Chip

*Kipper is the youngest in the family, he's 5 years old.*

Kipper

*Gran is always getting into trouble!*

Gran

*Floppy looks after the family.*

Floppy

**Biff, Chip and Kipper's friends:**

Wilf

Wilma

Nadim

Anneena

## The author-illustrator team

Author and illustrator team, Roderick Hunt and Alex Brychta, are two of the most experienced and successful reading scheme creators in the world. In 2008, Roderick Hunt received an MBE in the Queen's Birthday Honours List for services to education, particularly literacy. This was followed by further success when Roderick and Alex won the prestigious Outstanding Achievement Award at the Education Resources Awards 2009.

## Vocabulary and language development

The characters and action-packed illustrations in the *Sounds and Letters Books* and on the *Sounds and Letters* CD-ROM provide amazing scenarios for developing language comprehension. They bring the words to life, providing great stimulus for enriching vocabulary and developing speaking and listening skills.

The *Floppy's Phonics Sounds and Letters* programme provides all the instruction and practice children need to enable them to read *Floppy's Phonics Fiction* and *Non-fiction* before moving onto the rich variety of *Biff, Chip and Kipper Stories* in order to develop as confident and independent readers.

# Teaching children to read with synthetic phonics

## What is synthetic phonics?

The term 'synthetic phonics' refers to the process of synthesising, that is, blending the sounds of a word after sounding out the graphemes from left to right all the way through the word. This is 'decoding' from print to speech. For example:

To read the word 'hatch' we:

1. recognise the graphemes **h a tch**
2. translate the graphemes to phonemes (sounds) and say them aloud or silently **/h/ /a/ /ch/**
3. synthesise, or blend, the phonemes to hear the word '**hatch**'.

If a word is within the oral vocabulary of the reader, the decoding process will automatically activate the meaning of the word. Good alphabetic code knowledge and efficiency in the blending skill supports the comprehension of text.

We can identify around 44 phonemes in English speech, but have only 26 letters in the alphabet to represent those sounds for the writing process (encoding).

The English alphabetic code has many spelling alternatives (graphemes) as code for the sounds, and various graphemes can be pronounced in more than one way (pronunciation alternatives). For example, **ea** is pronounced differently in **ea**t, br**ea**d, br**ea**k.

For writing, we translate, or 'encode', the sounds of our speech into print. We orally split up (segment) the phonemes from beginning to end of spoken words and allocate each sound a letter or letter group.

### The synthetic phonics teaching principles

These include:

- the explicit and systematic teaching of the alphabetic code (the letter/s-sound correspondences);
- a focus on teaching the three core skills of blending for reading, segmenting for spelling, and handwriting;
- putting the alphabetic code knowledge taught to date and the three core skills to immediate use with cumulative, decodable words, sentences and texts.

## Cracking the code!

### Do you know your terminology?

**Blending:**
Identify the graphemes from left to right of the printed word, say the sounds and blend them to hear the whole word. (see page 26 for teaching tips)

The blending process is decoding.

**Segmenting:**
Identify the sounds from beginning to end of the spoken word. Write down a grapheme for each identified sound to spell the word.

The segmenting process is encoding.

In this programme we use the method of tallying sounds to your fingers to help children segment.

**Tips for spelling (encoding)**

Say the word slowly to identify each sound in the word.

Use your left hand to tally the individual sounds to your thumb and fingers.

Write down the letters or letter groups which are code for each sound you have tallied.

**Phoneme:**
The smallest identifiable sounds of speech.

**Grapheme:**
Letters or letter groups that are code for the focus sounds.

**Tricky words:**
Common words with unusual spellings which need special attention to note the tricky part e.g. the, one, once, of, who, are, their.

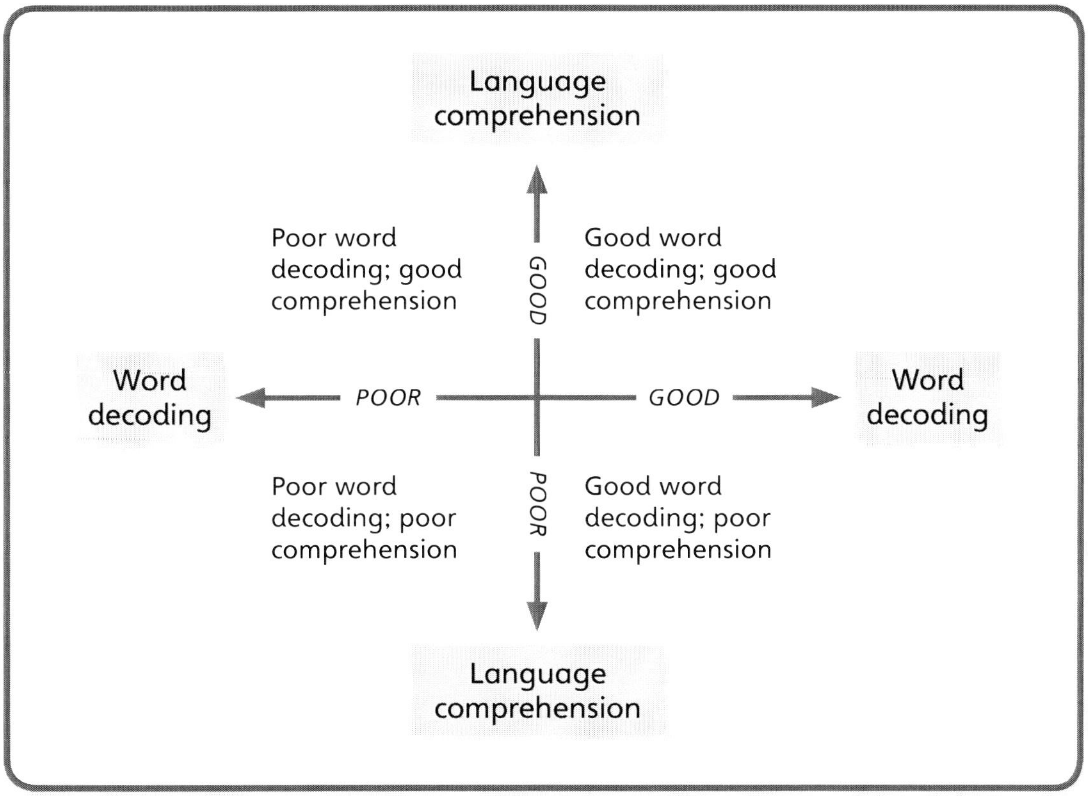


Gough and Tunmer's simple view of reading model (1986) was put forward in the *Independent review of the teaching of early reading* (*Final Report*, Jim Rose, March 2006) to show the need for readers to be proficient at word decoding as well as requiring good language comprehension.

# The alphabet and the alphabetic code

It is important to distinguish between the role of *the alphabet* and the role of *the alphabetic code*.

## How can the *Alphabet Poster* be used most effectively?

The *Alphabet Poster* provides a reference for writing the letter shapes. It introduces the concept of alphabetical order and introduces letter names. It needs to be on permanent display in an easy-to-see place.

### A bank of letter shapes for writing

- There are 26 pairs of letters (upper and lower case). In an infant-friendly font, there are only 6 identically-shaped letter pairs: Cc Oo Ss Vv Xx Zz. So, in real terms, learners have 46 discrete letter formations to learn along with their relative sizes and positions on a writing line.

### Sounds and letter names

- The *Alphabet Poster* can also be used to *say the sounds* of the individual letters as well as saying the names. Learn the names through chanting or singing an alphabet song at first, but use only sounds and not letter names for reading and oral segmenting.

### Upper case and lower case letters

- Learners need to see upper and lower case pairs together. It is possible that children may think of upper case letters by *name* and lower case letters by *sound* if it is not made clear that both the upper case letters and their lower case equivalent letters are code for the same sound.

### Alphabetical order

- Whilst the youngest learners are not ready to use dictionaries, or collate material alphabetically, they can be introduced to the usefulness of alphabetical order, for example, in the class register.

## How can the *Alphabetic Code Chart* be used most effectively?

An *Alphabetic Code Chart* is a very helpful teaching and learning tool. It clarifies understanding of the relationship between the sounds of our speech and the written code allotted to those sounds. The *Alphabetic Code Chart* displayed as a permanent resource supports both the planned step-by-step phonics teaching and incidental phonics teaching, as the need arises.

### Understanding the complexity of the alphabetic code

1) One sound (phoneme) can be represented by one, two, three or four letters, for example:

   /d/ as in **d**-o-g, /sh/ as in **sh**-i-p, /igh/ as in kn-**igh**-t, /oa/ as in d-**ough**

2) One sound can be represented by alternative spellings, for example:

| Different spellings of the long /oo/ sound | | | |
|---|---|---|---|
| sp**oo**n | cr**ew** | m**o**ve | s**ou**p |
| gl**ue** | fl**u**t**e** | fr**ui**t | s**u**perboy |

   Some spelling alternatives can be rare but appear in commonly used words.

3) One spelling can be code for alternative sounds, for example:

| Different pronunciations of the grapheme **ea** | | |
|---|---|---|
| /ee/ **ea**t | /e/ br**ea**d | /ai/ br**ea**k |

### Accents

People pronounce words very differently in different regions and countries. It is up to the teachers in those regions to take this into account when teaching phonics.

### Sounds

Sounds are written in slash marks. The choice of letter, or letters, used to represent the sounds within the slash marks depends upon how the letters work in common words, for example:

/k/ is used instead of /c/ because the letter **c** can represent more than one sound; **c** is the /k/ sound in **c**at, but it is the /s/ sound in **c**ity, whereas the letter **k** is consistently decoded as the /k/ sound in words. It is sensible, then, for /k/ rather than /c/ to denote the /k/ sound.

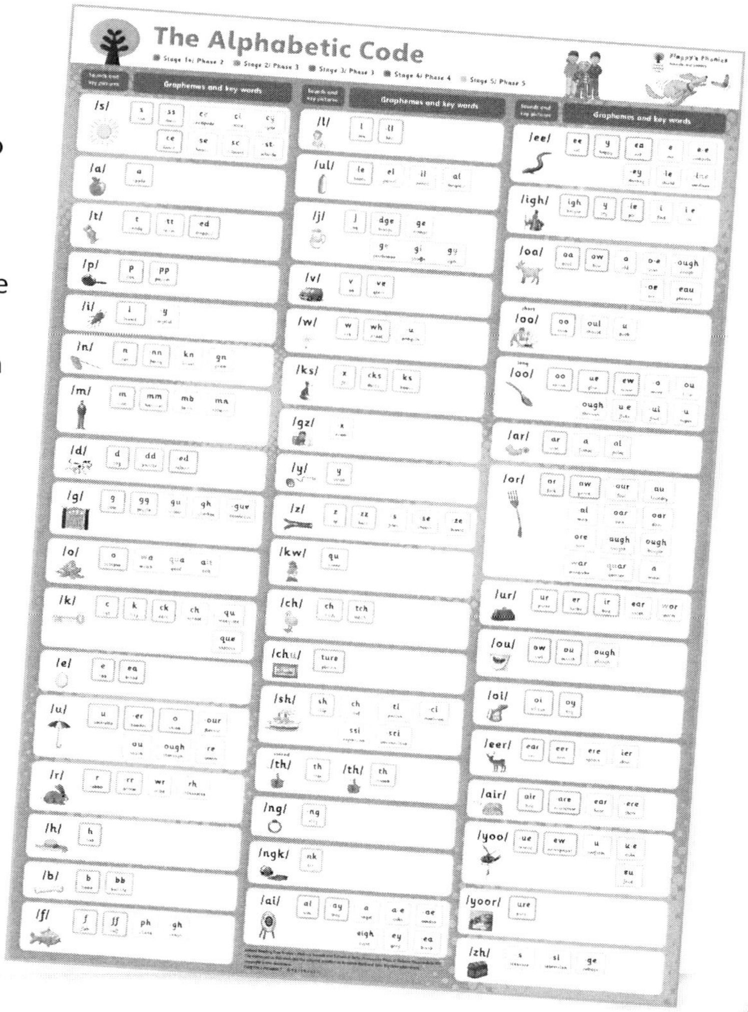

# A guide to the alphabetic code

## Vowel sounds

*Short* vowel sounds refer to:

| /a/ | /e/ | /i/ | /o/ | /u/ |
|---|---|---|---|---|
|  |  |  |  |  |
| as in **a**pple | as in **e**gg | as in **i**nsect | as in **o**ctopus | as in **u**mbrella. |

*Long* vowel sounds refer to the remaining vowel sounds:

| /ai/ | /ee/ | /igh/ | /oa/ | short /oo/ | long /oo/ | /ar/ | /or/ |
|---|---|---|---|---|---|---|---|
|  |  |  |  |  |  |  |  |
| **/ur/** | **/ou/** | **/oi/** | **/eer/** | **/air/** | **/yoo/** | **/yoor/** | |
|  |  |  |  |  |  |  | |

## What do the slashes mean?

Letters written like this /**k**/ refer to a sound, not a spelling.
e.g. /k/ as in **c**at, **k**ey, du**ck**

## What are the grey dashes?

Letter/s-sound correspondences which never *begin* a word are shown on the chart with a grey dash, such as -**ck**.

## Quick tips:

**/s/**

| | | | | |
|---|---|---|---|---|
| **s** sun | **-ss** dress | **ce** centipede | **ci** circle | **cy** cycle |
| **-ce** dance | **-se** house | **sc** scissors | **-st-** whistle | |

- Short words ending with the /s/ sound with *short* medial vowel sounds usually end with **ss** as in dre**ss**, ki**ss**, mo**ss** and fu**ss**. Look out for words spelled with medial **a** such as pa**ss**, as some people pronounce the **a** closer to *long* vowel sound /ar/; that is "p-*ar*-s" and this might mislead when spelling.
- Short words ending with the sounds /f/, /l/ and /z/ with *short* medial vowel sounds also end with double consonant letters **ff**, **ll** and **zz**.

**/g/**

| | | | | |
|---|---|---|---|---|
| **g** gate | **-gg** juggle | **gu** guitar | **gh** gherkin | **-gue** catalogue |

- Letter **u** in the grapheme **gu** acts as a block between the letter **g** and the letters **i**, **e** and **y**, indicating hard /g/ as in **gu**itar, **gu**est and **gu**y.

## /v/

| v | -ve |
|---|---|
| van | glove |

- Words ending with the /v/ sound are always spelled with the grapheme **ve** such as ha**ve**, gi**ve**, ser**ve**.
- Singular words ending with /f/ spelled with **f** (shel**f**, wol**f**, hoo**f**, lea**f**, el**f**, mysel**f**, cal**f**, hal**f**) when plural, change to /v+z/ and the spelling pattern **ves** (shel**ves**, wol**ves**, hoo**ves**, lea**ves**, el**ves**, oursel**ves**, cal**ves**, hal**ves**).

## /u/

| u | -er | o | -our |
|---|---|---|---|
| umbrella | builder | onion | flavour |

| -ou | -ough | -re |
|---|---|---|
| touch | thorough | centre |

- The very common *schwa effect* (unstressed syllable) is where various graphemes are pronounced by many people close to the /u/ sound in words such as build**er**, hum**our**, cent**re** and in other words such as **a**round, coll**ar**, sail**or**. Such words are easy to read and modify the pronunciation, but some are harder to recall the spelling.

## /ul/

| -le | -el | -il | -al |
|---|---|---|---|
| bottle | parcel | pencil | hospital |

- Teach the *schwa effect* in words such as bott**le**, parc**el**, penc**il**, anim**al** where **le**, **el**, **il**, **al** are pronounced close to /ul/. Literal sounding out when reading some words can help with recalling spelling alternatives such as a-n-i-m-**a**-l.

## /ks/

| -x | -cks | -ks |
|---|---|---|
| fox | ducks | books |

- **x** is code for two sounds /k/+/s/ but is taught as if it is one unit of sound /ks/. When /ks/ is identified through oral segmenting for spelling purposes, learners need to know that there are other ways to spell /ks/ as in boo**ks**, du**cks**, bi**kes**. This involves learning about singular/plural words and verb endings.

## /gz/

| -x |
|---|
| exam |

- The letter **x** is also code for two sounds /gz/, as in e**x**am, taught as if it is one unit of sound.

## /kw/

| qu |
|---|
| queen |

## /k/

| qu |
|---|
| mosquito |

- The letters **q** and **u** always appear together so they are introduced together as **qu**, at first as code for /kw/ as in **qu**een, and later as code for /k/ as in mos**qu**ito.

**/ng/** -ng ring **/ngk/** -nk ink

- The grapheme **ng** can be pronounced differently according to regional accents and dependent upon the particular word. In some words, the letters **n** and **g** are actually separate graphemes such as in d-a-**n**-**g**-er and j-u-**n**-**g**-le. In ju**n**gle, the **n** is code for /ng/.
- Teach **nk** as if it is one unit of sound for reading and spelling purposes even though it is really the two sounds /ng/+/k/. This works well for both early reading and spelling.

**/j/** j jug | -dge bridge | -ge orange

ge gentleman | gi giraffe | gy gym

- Words ending with the /j/ sound are spelled with **ge** (follows long vowel sounds or single consonant letters such as bar**ge**, spon**ge** and bul**ge**) or **dge** (follows short vowel sounds such as he**dge**, fu**dge**, do**dge**).
- When two-syllable words end with the sounds /i+j/, they are spelled with **age** such as vill**age**, pack**age**, rumm**age**.

**/ch/** ch chick | -tch hatch

- The grapheme **tch** is preceded by a *short* vowel sound, as in la**tch**, fe**tch**, pi**tch**, no**tch**, hu**tch**.
- The grapheme **ch** generally follows digraph *long* vowel sounds as in poa**ch**, rea**ch**, poo**ch**, ar**ch**, lur**ch**, por**ch**; and follows single consonant letters as in mul**ch** and pin**ch**.
- There are the common exception words, however, of su**ch**, mu**ch**, ri**ch**, whi**ch** and tou**ch** (*short* vowel sounds followed by **ch**).

## What do the grey letters mean?

The grey letters on the *Alphabetic Code Chart* and in the *Sounds and Letters Books* alert the reader to various pronunciations.

**/o/** o octopus | wa watch | qua quad | alt salt

- The graphemes **w** or **qu** preceding single letter **a** alert the reader that the letter **a** *might* be pronounced /o/. Compare w**a**tch with w**a**g; qu**a**d with qu**a**ck. Also, the letter pattern **alt** alerts the reader to pronounce the letter **a** as /o/ as in s**alt**.

## /s/

| | | | | | |
|---|---|---|---|---|---|
| s (sun) | -ss (dress) | ce (centipede) | ci (circle) | cy (cycle) | |
| | -ce (dance) | -se (house) | sc (scissors) | -st- (whistle) | |

## /k/

| | | | | |
|---|---|---|---|---|
| c (cat) | k (key) | -ck (duck) | ch (school) | qu (mosquito) |
| | | | | que (antique) |

- The letters **e**, **i** and **y** alert the reader that the preceding letter **c** is code for the /s/ sound. This is referred to as 'soft c', as in **c**entipede, **c**ircle, **c**ycle. This means that letter **c** is only code for the /k/ sound when it precedes letters **a**, **o** and **u** as in **c**at, **c**opy and **c**ubs.

## /j/

| | | | |
|---|---|---|---|
| j (jug) | -dge (bridge) | -ge (orange) | |
| | ge (gentleman) | gi (giraffe) | gy (gym) |

## /g/

| | | | | |
|---|---|---|---|---|
| g (gate) | -gg (juggle) | gu (guitar) | gh (gherkin) | -gue (catalogue) |

- The letters **e**, **i** or **y** alert the reader that the preceding letter **g** *might* be code for the /j/ sound. If so, it is referred to as 'soft g' as in **g**entleman, **g**iraffe, **g**ym. Otherwise, the sound for letter **g** remains 'hard' as in **g**ate and **g**oat; and in some words when **g** precedes **e**, **i** and **y**, such as **g**et, **g**iggle and fo**gg**y.

## /or/

| | | | |
|---|---|---|---|
| or (fork) | aw (yawn) | -our (four) | au (laundry) |
| | -al (walk) | oar (oars) | -oor (door) |
| | ore (sore) | -augh (caught) | ough (bought) |
| | war (wardrobe) | quar (quarter) | a (water) |

- The letter **w** preceding **ar** (war) alerts the reader to pronounce **ar** as /or/ as in w**ar**, w**ar**n, w**ar**ble, w**ar**drobe.
- The grapheme **qu** (/kw/) preceding **ar** also alerts the reader to pronounce **ar** as /or/ as in qu**ar**t, qu**ar**ter, qu**ar**tz.

# The structure of the Floppy's Phonics Sounds and Letters programme

| Letters and Sounds Phase | Oxford Reading Tree Stage | Floppy's Phonics Sounds and Letters Book | Sounds/ graphemes |
|---|---|---|---|
| Phase 1 | Stage 1 | At the Farm | environmental sounds |
| | | Out in Town | |
| | | Fun at School | |
| | | At Home | |
| | | At the Park | |
| | | At the Match | |
| Phase 2 | Stage 1+ | Book 1 | s a t p |
| | | Book 2 | i n m d |
| | | Book 3 | g o c k |
| | | Book 4 | ck e u r |
| | | Book 5 | h b f ff |
| | | Book 6 | l ll le ss |
| Phase 3 | Stage 2 | Book 7 | j v w |
| | | Book 8 | x y z |
| | | Book 9 | zz qu ch |
| | | Book 10 | sh th ng |
| | | Book 11 Revise and Stretch | dge ve wh |
| | | Book 12 Revise and Stretch | cks tch nk |
| | Stage 3 | Book 13 | ai ee igh |
| | | Book 14 | oa oo oo |
| | | Book 15 | ar or ur |
| | | Book 16 | ow oi ear |
| | | Book 17 | air er er |
| | | Book 18 Revise and Stretch | ue ue ure ture |

Phases 4 and 5 are listed in Handbook 2.

## What are the Revise and Stretch books?

These books revise familiar sounds and spellings of those sounds, and introduce one alternative spelling for the selected sounds. At Stage 2 the 'stretch' graphemes are alternative common consonant graphemes and at Stages 3 and 4 the focus is on alternative vowel graphemes. These spelling alternatives act as a stepping stone into Phase 5 and can provide children with the knowledge and skills to broaden their writing and reading experience.

# Helpful incidental phonics teaching tips

These five incidental early teaching tips are important to teach alongside the structured learning of the alphabetic code and handwriting. This enables some children to read a wider variety of texts and supports their early writing. Some children may have advanced skills and benefit from this level of incidental teaching at an early stage to address their special needs.

1. **Encountering e at the end of words**

   Right from the start, point out that many printed words in English end with letter **e**. Teach the children not to sound out the 'end **e**' in words.

   In some words this 'end **e**' alerts readers to decode the words with *long vowel* sounds (e.g. m**a**k**e** is /m/ /ai/ /k/, not /m/ /a/ /k/). But not all words with 'end **e**' are split digraph words, so take care to point this out to children (e.g. have).

2. **Introducing short and long vowel sounds**

   Once the single vowel letters **a**, **e**, **i**, **o**, **u** are introduced as code for the *short* vowel sounds of /a/, /e/, /i/, /o/, /u/ (as in **a**pple, **e**gg, **i**nsect, **o**ctopus and **u**mbrella), start to teach incidentally that these single letters can also be code for the *long* vowel sounds of /ai/, /ee/, /igh/, /oa/ and /yoo/ (as in **a**ngel, m**e**, f**i**nd, **o**ld and **u**niform).

   For reading, teach, "If blending with the *short* vowel sound does not make a real word, try blending again with the *long* vowel sound." This creates a very flexible reader who understands that the decoding process needs to be addressed with common sense and without being afraid of getting it wrong.

3. **Tweaking sounds as you blend**

   Teaching the notion of modifying pronunciation after blending will address many words such as o**f**, ha**s**, i**s**, th**e**, p**u**t and p**u**ll. For example, when has is sounded out it should lead to 'hass' which is modified to 'haz'.

4. **Encountering double consonant letters**

   Teach the children to say only one sound when they encounter double consonant letters, e.g. la**dd**er. The graphemes **ss**, **ll**, **ff** and **zz** are taught as special cases for spelling purposes, not for reading.

   Children can learn that double consonant letters (including **ck**) are always preceded by single letter short vowel sounds (see point 2).

5. **Encountering ed, er and y endings**

   Once letters **e** and **d** have been introduced, then you can start to draw attention to them in wider reading and model them in writing when they are used as **ed** verb endings.

   This addresses **ed** verb endings as code for the sounds:
   /d/ as in rain**ed**; /t/ as in dropp**ed**; /e+d/ as in decod**ed**

   It is also helpful to address **er** endings and **y** endings incidentally as they are so common:
   /u/ as in build**er**; /ee/ as in happ**y**; /igh/ as in cr**y**

# The Floppy's Phonics mnemonic system

*Floppy's Phonics Sounds and Letters* has a colourful, child-friendly, mnemonic system based on key exemplar words and pictures. At first the key pictures act as prompts to recall the sounds linked to the letter shapes.

Wherever possible, at the beginning stages of learning the alphabetic code, the focus sound is the *first sound* of the key word, for example, /s/ **s**un, /a/ **a**pple, /t/ **t**eddy. Children see the letter shape and say the sound prompted by the key picture. Children are only expected to read the focus grapheme in black, not the whole word. By seeing the focus grapheme in the context of a whole word (the focus grapheme in black and the rest of the word in grey) children can link the position of the focus grapheme in the written word to when they hear, or say, the focus sound in the spoken word.

Mnemonic systems are helpful and motivating, but require careful use so that children are not dependent, for example, on picture cues and directional arrows, and the system must not detract from core learning. From the outset of this programme, letters are provided repeatedly with **no picture cues**, such as on the back of the *Flashcards*, the Activity Sheets and in the 'Say the sounds' strips in the *Sounds and Letters Books*, along the bottom of the CD-ROM spreads and on the photocopiable Say the Sounds Posters and Grapheme Tiles.

The key pictures and key words are consistent across all of the resources. There are also small black and white line versions of the key pictures for colouring-in on the Activity Sheets and Grapheme Tiles for home.

## Stage 1+ key words and key pictures

| sound | grapheme | key picture | key word |
|---|---|---|---|
| /s/ | s |  | **s**un |
| /a/ | a |  | **a**pple |
| /t/ | t |  | **t**eddy |
| /p/ | p |  | **p**an |
| /i/ | i |  | **i**nsect |
| /n/ | n | 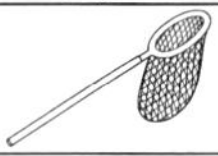 | **n**et |
| /m/ | m |  | **m**an |
| /d/ | d |  | **d**og |
| /g/ | g |  | **g**ate |
| /o/ | o |  | **o**ctopus |

| | | | |
|---|---|---|---|
| /k/ | c |  | cat |
| /k/ | k |  | key |
| /k/ | -ck |  | duck |
| /e/ | e | 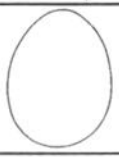 | egg |
| /u/ | u |  | umbrella |
| /r/ | r |  | rabbit |
| /h/ | h |  | hat |
| /b/ | b |  | bone |
| /f/ | f |  | fish |
| /f/ | -ff | 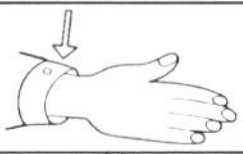 | cuff |
| /l/ | l |  | lion |
| /l/ | -ll |  | hill |
| /ul/ | -le |  | bottle |
| /s/ | -ss |  | dress |

## Stage 2 key words and key pictures

| sound | grapheme | key picture | key word |
|---|---|---|---|
| /j/ | j |  | jug |
| /v/ | v |  | van |
| /w/ | w | 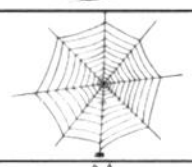 | web |
| /ks/ | -x |  | fox |
| /y/ | y | 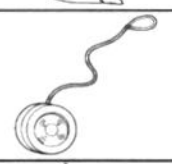 | yo-yo |
| /z/ | z |  | zip |
| /z/ | -zz |  | buzz |
| /kw/ | qu |  | queen |
| /ch/ | ch |  | chick |
| /sh/ | sh |  | ship |

| | | | |
|---|---|---|---|
| voiced /th/ and unvoiced /th/ | th |  | this thumb |
| /ng/ | -ng |  | ring |
| /j/ | -dge |  | bridge |
| /v/ | -ve | 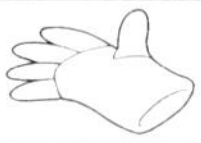 | glove |
| /w/ | wh |  | wheel |
| /ks/ | -cks |  | ducks |
| /ch/ | -tch |  | hatch |
| /ngk/ | -nk |  | ink |

## Stage 3 key words and key pictures

| sound | grapheme | key picture | key word |
|---|---|---|---|
| /ai/ | ai |  | aim |
| /ee/ | ee | 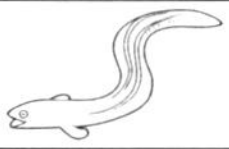 | eel |
| | -y |  | happy |
| /igh/ | -igh |  | knight |
| | -y |  | cry |
| /oa/ | oa |  | goat |
| short /oo/ | -oo |  | cook |
| long /oo/ | oo |  | spoon |
| /ar/ | ar |  | arm |
| /or/ | or |  | fork |
| /ur/ | ur |  | purse |
| /ou/ | ow |  | owl |
| /oi/ | oi | 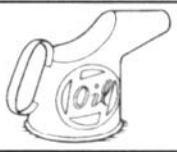 | oil can |

| | | | |
|---|---|---|---|
| /eer/ | **ear** |  | **ear** |
| /air/ | **air** |  | h**air** |
| /u/ | -**er** |  | build**er** |
| /ur/ | **er** |  | h**er**bs |
| /yoo/ | -**ue** |  | resc**ue** |
| long /oo/ | -**ue** |  | gl**ue** |
| /yoor/ | -**ure** |  | p**ure** |
| /chu/ | -**ture** |  | pic**ture** |

## Mnemonics for spelling

The key pictures and words not only provide fun, initial memory-triggers for recalling the **sounds**, but as the programme progresses they also provide a reference system for the **spelling alternatives** of the sounds. The key pictures and words enable the teacher and children to talk in the shared language of, "You need the spelling of /ee/ as in shield, not /ee/ as in eel". The *Alphabetic Code Chart* features the key pictures for the sounds and key words for the graphemes (spelling alternatives) across the rows.

In Stage 1+, children are introduced to these alternative spellings:
/k/ as in **c**at, **k**ey and du**ck**; /f/ as in **f**ish and cu**ff**; /l/ as in **l**ion and hi**ll** (and /ul/ as in bott**le**); /s/ as in **s**un and dre**ss**.

This programme also introduces these common alternative spellings through the 'Revise and Stretch' books at Stage 2 and Stage 3:
/j/ as in **j**ug and bri**dge**
/v/ as in **v**an and glo**ve**
/w/ as in **w**eb and **wh**eel
/x/ as in fo**x** and du**cks**
/ch/ as in **ch**ick and ha**tch**
/ng/ as in ri**ng** and /ngk/ as in i**nk**

It is quite challenging to learn which words are spelled with which spelling alternatives, so gradually introducing children to the concept of alternative spellings helps to prepare them for Stage 5 (Phase 5) and will increase their opportunities for further reading at home and at school along the way.

Teaching spelling should not be perceived as boring or hard work, neither should it switch to becoming 'Look, Cover, Write, Check'. Bring a touch of magic and enthusiasm to the lessons by various challenges such as: story-writing, spelling bees, handwriting, reading stories aloud and acting out spelling word banks as clues for other classes to deduce then recall. Ultimately, for spelling, children need to commit a number of spelling word banks to long term memory (e.g. words with the /k/ sound ad the **ch** spelling, such as **ch**aos, **ch**orus, s**ch**ool and **ch**emist).

# Establishing good routines

## Why are good routines important?

Children respond well to routines and they thrive on the kind of classroom management where they:

- share collective procedures, such as very quickly and quietly gathering on the carpet with established seating positions 'ready for learning'
- know that they can focus fully on their own work – confident in what this will consist of and recognise that they are making good progress.

Good routines are essential for phonics teaching as there is a lot of alphabetic code knowledge to teach to the children. The more simple, efficient and disciplined the teaching routines, the greater the likelihood the slower-to-learn children will engage with the learning, enabling them to keep up, and the more likely that all the children will enjoy the lessons and gain maximum knowledge.

## Recommended simple teaching routines

This programme's terminology does not refer to *sound buttons*, and dots and dashes are not provided beneath printed words. There are no robot-arms actions, or robot voices, and no counting sounds involved with the reading process. The reading, spelling and writing routines described below are simple, focused, appropriate and repeated.

### A routine for blending:

- Finger-track under the graphemes of each word from left to right with the index finger of the child's writing hand, whilst saying the sounds.
- After saying the sounds one at a time, return the index finger to under the first grapheme and run the finger under the whole word whilst saying the whole blended word.
- Modify the pronunciation of the blended word if necessary.

## Debbie Hepplewhite's Top Tips

**What is blending?**
For reading (decoding) say the sounds from left to right of the word and blend the sounds to hear the whole word.

**How to blend:**
Point under each letter as you say the sound, then run your finger under the whole word as you say the whole (or blended) word.

e.g. **y-e-s** **yes**

**Tips for spelling (encoding)**
Say the word slowly to identify each sound in the word.

Use your left hand to tally the individual sounds to your thumb and fingers.

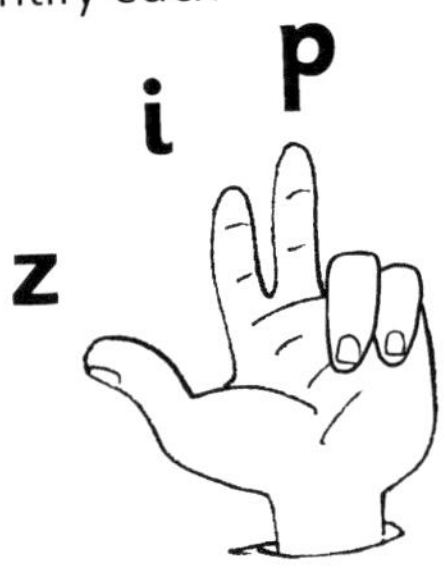


Write down the letters and letter groups which are code for each sound you have tallied.

### A routine for segmenting:

- Orally segment words by saying the words slowly (enabling the individual sounds and mouth shapes to be clearly evident) whilst tallying each sound to your thumb and fingers of your left hand.

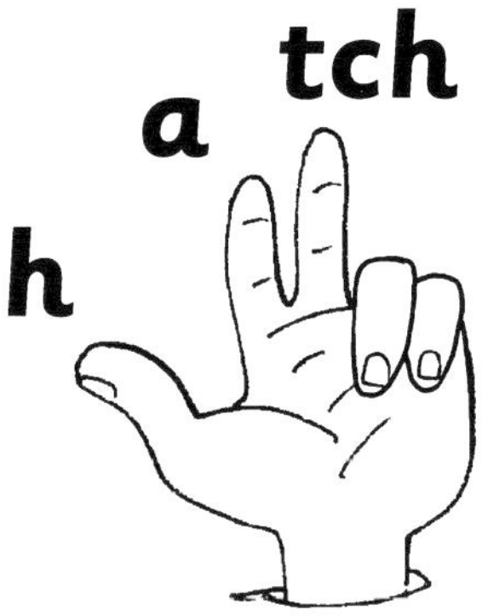


- Draw sound dashes (writing lines) for the sounds counted on thumb and fingers during the routine above and select small Grapheme Tiles for the identified sounds to place on the sound dashes from left to right. Alternatively, write the graphemes straight onto the sound dashes.

  **h a tch ✓**

- Check, or edit, the proposed spelling by sounding out and blending the selected graphemes (again with finger-tracking). Ask the children to make corrections as necessary. Encourage children to tick correct spellings.

The sound dashes provide a temporary stepping-stone for spelling. When the children can write beyond word level, they can orally segment and write their spellings without the sound dashes.

### A routine for handwriting:

- Finger-trace letter shapes and air-write with the index finger of the child's writing hand and say the sounds at the same time.
- Hold pencils correctly with the tripod pencil grip (shown right).

### Routines to learn the letter/s–sound correspondences of the alphabetic code include:

- pointing to individual graphemes to 'say the sounds' (in the order you have introduced them and then randomly)
- saying the sounds to the children and asking them to point to the graphemes (e.g. "Point to /s/, /t/, /a/, /n/. Point to /k/ as in **cat** and then /k/ as in **duck**").

The *Flashcards*, *Frieze*, *Books*, CD-ROM and *Posters* all support these routines and allow variation in how the routines can be practised in the classroom.

# The two-session approach

The resources are designed to be delivered in two distinct sessions so that the children can enjoy the benefits of collective whole-class teaching, followed by opportunities where they are able to fully concentrate on their own learning. They can also be used flexibly and discretely as required.

- **Session 1** is approximately a 30 minute teacher-led session focusing on the introduction of sounds and graphemes, as well as modelling and practising the skills of blending, segmenting and handwriting, using the *Flashcards*, *Frieze* and CD-ROM on the Interactive Whiteboard.
- **Session 2** is a longer session that provides a revise-and-apply routine where children focus on their own learning at their own level, using the *Sounds and Letters Books*, the Activity Sheets and the extension Cumulative Texts (with the teacher drawing the attention of the whole class together as needed).

The alternating second session of the phonics lessons can take place later in the day or the next day, or as an immediate follow-on, if preferred, once the routines are established. In this way, every child benefits from the activity.

Time spent on phonics will vary depending on the time available and the children's needs and stage of learning. This step-by-step lesson structure offers a guide for how to use the resources to their full potential, but they can also be used flexibly to suit your needs. The *Planning and Assessment* CD-ROM provides plans to organise your phonics sessions. These can be edited and customised.

| | |
|---|---|
| **Revisit and Review**<br>Revise sounds and graphemes with the *Flashcards* and the *Frieze*. | **Session 1** |
| **Teach**<br>Teach focus sounds and graphemes using the *Flashcards* and the *Sounds and Letters* CD-ROM. | |
| **Practise**<br>Practise new and revised sounds and graphemes with the *Sounds and Letters Books* and the *Sounds and Letters* Activity Sheets. | **Session 2** |
| **Apply**<br>After the focus sound and grapheme is taught, use the Cumulative Texts for grapheme searches, reading and handwriting practice and use the Grapheme Tiles for spelling practice. | |
| **Consolidate**<br>Use the *Sounds and Letters Books* and the CD-ROM activities for revision and to consolidate learning. | **For further practice and/or extension** |
| **Further phonics practice**<br>Read *Floppy's Phonics Fiction* and *Non-fiction*. | |

# A step-by-step example lesson for Stages 1+, 2 and 3

### Teach the /p/ sound (Stage 1+/Phase 2)

## Session 1

### Revisit and Review

This part of the lesson should be done at a quick pace, to review previously introduced graphemes and sounds.

- **Say the sounds**: Hold up the *Flashcards* **(s a t)** one by one in any order and ask the children to say the sounds (not the key words). The ultimate aim of the activity is that the children can 'say the sounds' in response to the graphemes on the back of the cards, with no picture clue.
- **Hear the sounds and point to the graphemes**: Using the *Frieze*, say the sounds previously introduced in a jumbled order and ask the children to point to the corresponding graphemes.

### Teach

**Teach the new sound and grapheme with the *Flashcards*:**

- **Teach the new sound and grapheme:** Show the class the *Flashcard* for the new sound and grapheme (e.g. /p/ p). Say the sound several times encouraging the children to repeat after you. Ask them if it is a loud or a quiet sound (vowel sounds provide the volume in words, consonant sounds are quiet). Say the picture-word (pan) and ask children to listen for where they can hear the focus sound (at the beginning). Explain to the children that remembering the key picture can help them to remember the new sound.

**Teach the new sound and grapheme with the CD-ROM (See User Guide for full details):**

- Bring up the spread on the CD-ROM for the new sound/grapheme (e.g. /p/ Pp) on the Interactive Whiteboard (IWB).
- Ask the children to point to the new grapheme and say the new sound. Select the audio icon to see if they were correct.
- Point to the key picture (e.g. **p**an) and ask the children to say the word and repeat where they can hear the new sound in the word. Select to hear the sound and key word (/p/ pan).
- Point to the capital letter and remind them that it is code for the same sound as the lower case letter.
- **Modelling handwriting**: Select the letters to play the writing animation showing the directionality of the letter formations. The children can watch at first and then join in by air-writing the graphemes.
- **Modelling blending**: Select the first word in the cumulative word list. Select the individual graphemes to hear the sounds and then select **blend** to see and hear the word blended. Where **reveal** appears on the screen, this can be selected to display a picture showing children the meaning of the word.

- **Speaking and listening and comprehension**: Now focus on the main illustration on the whiteboard. Tell the children to turn to their partner to talk about the characters in the picture – who they are and how they are feeling related to what is happening.
- **Phonemic awareness**: Explain that, as a class, you are going to look for 2 or 3 words in the picture with the new sound (e.g. /p/). Select the audio icons on the illustration and ask the children to listen for the new sound in the spoken words. Point to 1 or 2 pictures of words that do not include the focus sound to check that the children are listening for the correct sound.
- **Modelling spelling**: Choose a word from the back of the *Flashcard* for the new sound/grapheme. Say the word very slowly and as naturally as possible, so that all the mouth movements are evident and all the individual sounds can be heard (e.g. t-a-p). Model how to tally the sounds to the thumb and fingers of your left hand, palm facing. [See page 13 of this handbook for the routine]
- Repeat the tallying but this time orally segment the word as clear, discrete sounds (e.g. /t/ /a/ /p/). After tallying, count the number of thumb and fingers raised, (three) to indicate the three sounds in the word.
- Using the Grapheme Tiles, the *Flashcards* or the *Frieze*, ask children to point to the correct graphemes that represent the sounds in the word you've just tallied to your left hand.

  From *Book 1 spread 3* onwards, you can model how to use the 'Drag and drop' spelling activities on the CD-ROM to practise spelling. Select the **Chip** icon at the bottom right of the screen and a new window will open up. See the CD-ROM User Guide for detailed instructions.

## Session 2

### Practise

Practise using the *Sounds and Letters Books*:

- Tell the children to open their books to the right page (e.g. page 8 for /p/ Pp).
- Ask the children if anyone remembers the sound they learned in the previous session (e.g. /p/).
- Point to the capital letter and remind them that it is code for the same sound as the lower case letter but used for names, etc.
- Tell them to finger-trace the letter shapes and to say the sound.
- Point to the 'Say the sounds' strip at the foot of the spread and ask the children to point to the letters and say the sounds in order. Then ask them to point to the sounds in a jumbled order and say the sounds.
- Ask the children to point to the first word in the cumulative word list. Remind them to use their index finger of their writing hand to point under each letter from left to right whilst sounding out (e.g. /p/ /a/ /t/). Remind them to return their finger to under the first letter and then run the finger under the whole word whilst saying the whole, blended word. After giving them a chance to blend the word themselves, repeat the process together. Ask them what the word means.

- Ask them to look at the rest of the words in the list and to sound out the letters and blend the sounds to read the words aloud to themselves. Repeat the sounding out and blending of this list of words as a group.
- Encourage the children to talk about the characters and events in the picture. Can they remember any new words (vocabulary) which were introduced in the previous session?

- Point to the labels on the main illustration one at a time and ask the children to look at what the label refers to (e.g. a pot). Ask the children to say the word and look at the focus letter shape in the label. Notice the relationship between the focus sound and letter and their relative positions in the spoken and printed words (beginning, middle or end).
- Ask the children to look for any other items in the illustration (two or three) that include the focus sound, like they did as a class in the previous session. Examples of these are given at the foot of the page for the adult's reference.

### Practise using the Activity Sheets:

Train all the children thoroughly in how to proceed through the activities on the Activity Sheets. Once children know how to do this, then most of them will be able to proceed independently. This enables any supervising adults to focus on the slower-to-learn children.

- **Learning the letter/s-sound correspondence**: Ask the children to say the sound and trace the letter(s) with their index finger.
- Encourage the children to look at the picture and say the word, while listening out for the focus sound. They can colour the picture after completing the sheet.
- **Practising blending**: Encourage the children to read the words by sounding out and blending the sounds to themselves. For the first few Activity Sheets this section includes single letters to sound out first, before moving on to blending full words.
- **Vocabulary**: Ask the children to tick each word they think they have blended correctly and circle any word they have blended where they do not know the meaning of the word. Tick any word that you hear being blended correctly by the child.
- **Handwriting**: When undertaking the handwriting routines, teach the children to say the sound of the grapheme (letter or letter group) and not the individual letter names. Model how to hold their pencils correctly in the tripod pencil grip (see p27).
- **Articulation and phonemic awareness**: Ask the children to look at the pictures at the bottom of the sheet and ask them to say what the words are to themselves and to listen for the focus sound. The pictures have been selected to show the focus sound in different positions.

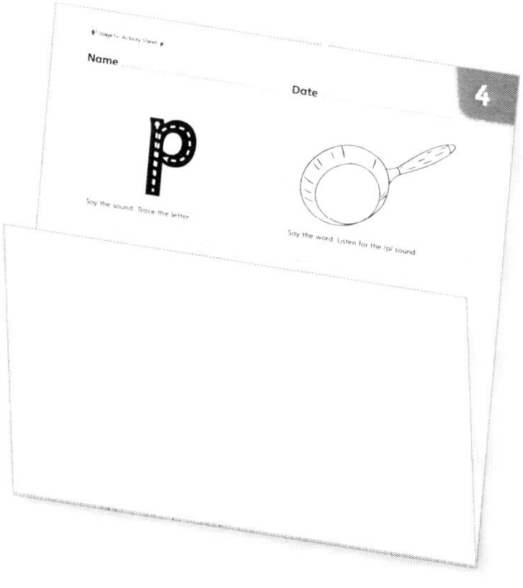


- **Linking focus sound to drawing**: For the final independent activity on the front of the Activity Sheet, ask the children to choose a word with the focus sound in it and to draw a simple picture of it in the space provided.
- **Supported spelling**: Show children how to fold up their Activity Sheets to just under the focus grapheme and ask children to copy the new letter on the back of the Activity Sheet, using the directional arrows to help them. After a short while, you can provide words, said slowly, for the children to undertake the spelling-with-editing routine on the folded up part of the Activity Sheet.

## Apply

### Apply using the Cumulative Texts:

- For every new sound and grapheme introduced (from *Book 3* onwards), there are corresponding Cumulative Texts. Photocopy the Cumulative Text in advance from the *Planning, Assessment and Resources Book* and have them ready to use for children who finish first or for a whole group.
- Train the children to scan through the words and underline any focus graphemes for a 'grapheme search'. Ask them to read the text, blending any words they do not know.

### Apply using the Grapheme Tiles:

- For spelling practice activities, you can use the Grapheme Tiles. These are photocopiable in the *Planning, Assessment and Resources Book* (pages 90–98). Photocopy all the relevant graphemes they have learned to date.
- Using the back of the *Flashcards* (or Activity Sheets) for your cumulative word bank, say a word and ask the children to repeat the word to themselves slowly, then to orally segment the word whilst tallying the sounds to their thumb and fingers as per the routine.
- Support the children as necessary to achieve the right number of sounds, then ask them to look at the Grapheme Tiles spread out on their tables. Ask them to identify which of the letters in front of them is code for the first sound. Repeat this for each of the sounds until they have spelled the full word. Finally, ask them to sound out and blend the word to check that it is correct.

## Consolidate

### Consolidate using the *Sounds and Letters Books*:

- Once you have taught all the new sounds and graphemes in each of the Books, work on the consolidation and practice activities at the back of the *Sounds and Letters Books*.
- Firstly, ask the children to look at pages 10 and 11 and to finger-trace the letters. Then ask them to look at the pictures on page 11 and to say the words the pictures represent.
- Secondly, ask them to use the 'Say the sounds' sound strips to revise the sounds they have learned so far.
- Finally, ask them to look at page 12 and focus on matching the upper and lower case versions of each letter. Then ask them to look at the bottom of the page and to sound out and blend the words to read them.

### Consolidate using the *Sounds and Letters CD-ROM:*

You can also set the children up with the CD-ROM. Encourage them to use the audio and interactive activities to practise the sounds and graphemes they have learned so far. Use the 'say the sounds' audio and the jumble activity to practise the letter/s-sound correspondences. The audio facility on the main illustrations are very helpful to improve vocabulary of spoken English for children with speech difficulties and with English as an additional language.

Whilst you are teaching the Stage 1+ *Sounds and Letters Books*, display the Say the Sounds Poster for Stage 1+ where children will frequently see it, e.g. by their coats. Use it to 'say the sounds' and 'point to the graphemes' in response to someone else who says the sounds as often as possible.

# Grouping

All children need to learn the same alphabetic code knowledge and three core skills. *Floppy's Phonics Sounds and Letters* resources are designed with differentiation and special needs in mind, making the grouping of children using the programme surprisingly simple.

- **Session I is teacher-led and is a whole class activity.**

  The teacher needs to ensure that slower-to-learn and less attentive children have a very clear view of the Interactive Whiteboard and the teacher, and that they are actively engaged throughout the lesson.

  When selecting children to do an activity on the IWB, find ways to engage the other children kinaesthetically from their sitting positions. Allow some, or all, of them to stand up occasionally when air-writing, saying the sounds, pointing to the graphemes, and when pointing to the graphemes whilst blending collectively.

- **Session 2 is a pupil activity session**, children will need to be grouped according to how many books and adult staff you have available.

  Children do *not* need to be grouped by ability. There is sufficient differentiation built into the resources and guidance for children to know what to do if they have worked more quickly than others. They may proceed, for example, with their Cumulative Text if they have completed the Activity Sheet and are waiting for the words for the spelling-with-editing routine to be provided. Alternatively, they may have a reading book to enjoy.

  It may be appropriate to organise a group of children who are slower to learn who will, at first, look at the *Sounds and Letters Book* in a group with a supervising adult. The remainder of the children form a second group who start completing their Activity Sheets independently.

No different resources need to be prepared for individual children although individuals may need additional time for revision of past and recent lessons or individual extension activities. Cumulative Texts, Grapheme Tiles, the CD-ROM and Activity Sheets are perfect resources to provide extra practice and extension.

# Differentiation

## Same code, same skills, same resources

Whatever the children's maturity, ability, and stage of learning, it is the *same* alphabetic code and three core skills that need to be taught.

## Words of different lengths from the outset

There are words of different lengths and structures across the *Sounds and Letters* programme from the outset to provide for all children. There is no need to create multiple ability groups in the class.

The *Sounds and Letters Books*, provide a 'stretch word' on every spread to allow children to extend their blending skills.

The posters also expose all children to a range of words and the entire alphabetic code giving the bigger picture.

You can never tell when children will make the next leap of learning. It does not matter if some children are still at the stage of using printed words simply to 'say the sounds' whilst their peers are able to blend those same words.

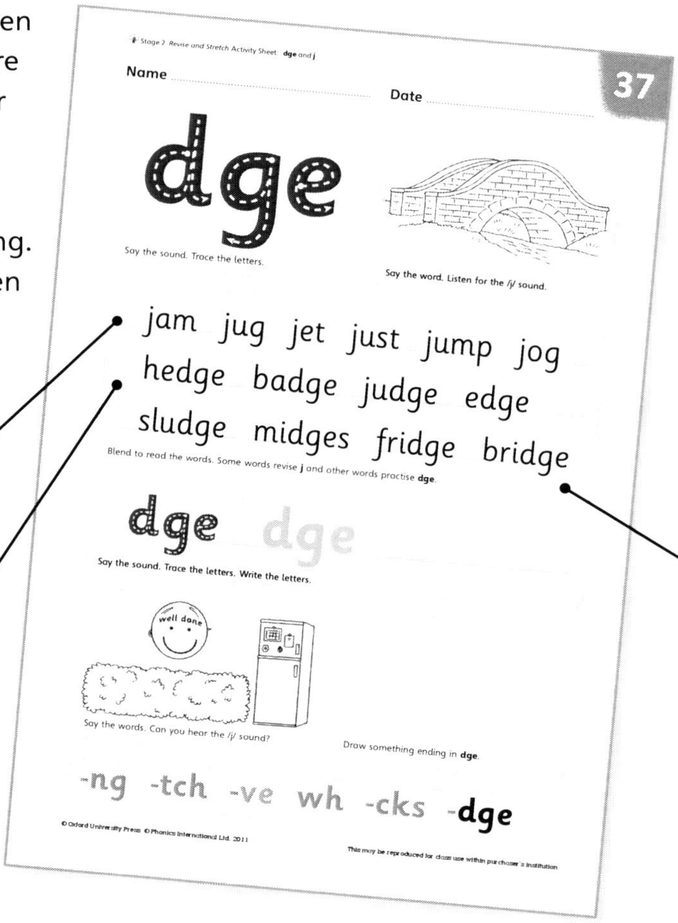
Stage 2 Revise and Stretch Activity Sheet: dge and j

Name ............ Date ............ 37

dge

Say the sound. Trace the letters.

Say the word. Listen for the /j/ sound.

jam jug jet just jump jog
hedge badge judge edge
sludge midges fridge bridge

Blend to read the words. Some words revise j and other words practise dge.

dge dge

Say the sound. Trace the letters. Write the letters.

well done

Say the words. Can you hear the /j/ sound?

Draw something ending in dge.

-ng -tch -ve wh -cks -dge

© Oxford University Press © Phonics International Ltd. 2011

This may be reproduced for class use within purchaser's institution

The *Activity Sheets* provide sounding out and blending practice at various levels and provide extension for those who need it.

Some children may be at the stage of simply 'saying the sounds' for these words.

Some children may be able to blend most or all of these words.

Some children may be able to blend some of these words

### Individual learning pace

Whilst all the children use the same resources, they will access this material at their own level of understanding. Children who are quicker to learn can continue with extension work using the Cumulative Texts (handwriting on lines, self-dictation, write next sentence), Grapheme Tiles and CD-ROM activities, other children may use them at a later date.

### Good training

All the children can be very well-trained in the routines and requirements of using familiar resources. These routines encourage consistent behaviour and allow the groups to work without complicated ability streaming.

### Slip between whole class, group and individual teaching during the lessons

Periodically, during session 2, draw the attention of the whole class together to summarise the various sections of the Activity Sheets. For example, to discuss any new vocabulary in the word lists, to provide the words for the spelling-with-editing routine on the folded-up part of the sheet, or simply to recognise children who have worked independently and deserve some immediate feedback and appreciation.

## Special educational needs

The *Floppy's Phonics Sounds and Letters* resources cater for all needs of children. They are carefully coordinated to provide daily, precise and explicit step-by-step teaching, with repetition and revision for all children including those who, for whatever reason, are often left behind in whole class scenarios or who simply need more time to embed learning and concepts to long-term memory.

Synthetic phonics longitudinal studies have shown that boys do as well, or better, than girls, and that younger children do as well as older children in the same cohort, as do children for whom English is an additional language. Synthetic phonics is particularly essential for children with dyslexia and any intervention should take the form of additional teaching and learning opportunities in the *Floppy's Phonics Sounds and Letters* programme and the synthectic phonics teaching principles rather than a change of teaching programme and methods.

### Children with advanced knowledge and skills

Some children may come to school already knowing at least some of the letter/s-sound correspondences, or names of some letters, and they may even have begun to read and write. They are unlikely to be proficient in all aspects of reading, spelling and handwriting and such children are still well-served by a complete synthetic phonics programme starting from the beginning.

It is often a good strategy to facilitate children with opportunities at the end of phonics lessons to read and write freely (and at other times) and to take home free-choice reading books in addition to the more structured reading books.

# Home–school partnerships

The more your school informs parents and succeeds in encouraging them to support the learning, the greater the benefits for the children themselves and the school. If individual children are slower-to-learn and struggle to learn, parental support can be significantly beneficial.

## Informing parents before school starts

Ideally, parents of children who are new to the setting will already be aware that the school is using the *Floppy's Phonics Sounds and Letters* programme to teach the alphabetic code and skills for reading, spelling and writing. A draft letter to parents is provided on page 38 and the school could mention the use of the *Floppy's Phonics* programme through its literacy policy, in the school prospectus, via the school website and during the general 'welcome to the school' information evening.

## Once their child has started school

- At an early stage in the school year, the school could provide an additional Parents' Information Evening to explain how reading, spelling and writing is taught. Demonstrate the phonics routines, and describe how the lessons provide for the differing needs of children, how reading books are assigned to the children and point to the guidance for parents on the inside covers of the books. Make the event interactive, and require the parents to 'say the sounds' cleanly (that is, say "sss" and not "suh"), to complete an Activity Sheet and to undertake the blending, oral segmenting and spelling routines (page 26). Encourage parents to make shared reading at home a positive and enjoyable experience, as this will undoubtedly increase their child's confidence in school.
- Suggest to parents how teaching staff and parents can write simple messages in the children's reading record books to share information for the children's benefit.
- Display a copy of the *Alphabetic Code Chart* in the school foyer as a permanent reference chart for visiting parents and general visitors.
- Invite the school's governors to attend the Parents' Information Evening and ensure that all governors are aware of the school's approach to basic literacy.

## Resources to help parents support their child at home

- ***Floppy's Phonics Sounds and Letters***
  The resources that you use in class can be sent home for extra practice, consolidation or extension: Activity Sheets, Books, Grapheme and Picture Tiles for home, Cumulative Texts, Say the Sounds Posters.

- **Letters and guidance sheets for parents**
  These have been designed to make informing parents quick and easy, and to help you give them the support they need to use the materials, such as the *Grapheme* and *Picture Tiles* at home.

  These can be found on page 38 of this *Sounds and Letters Handbook* and pages 99–117 of the *Planning, Assessment and Resources* book and CD-ROM.

- **Inside cover notes**
  All *Oxford Reading Tree* books provide guidance for parents and carers in the inside cover notes.

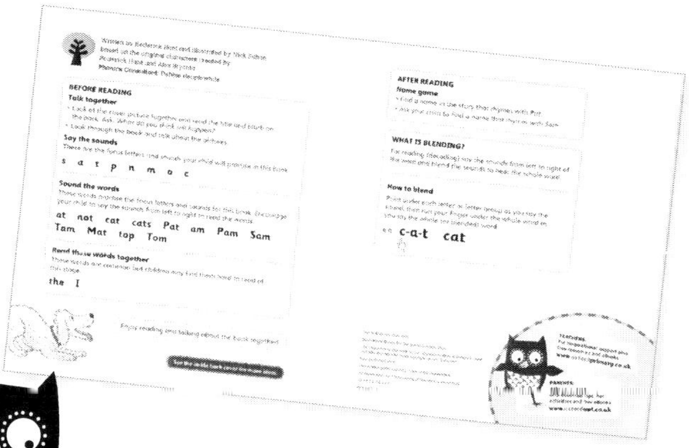


- **The Oxford Owl website:** *www.oxfordowl.co.uk*
  This website provides essential tips, phonics support and free eBooks for parents and children.

  It includes the following, and much more:
  - how to pronounce pure sounds
  - information about phonics
  - advice on how to share a book
  - free activities
  - free eBooks

- ***Floppy's Phonics Fiction* and *Non-fiction***
  These exciting Biff, Chip and Kipper stories and fact books are fully decodable and matched to the *Letters and Sounds* progression. They are perfect for decoding practice and for increasing children's confidence and fluency, and have support for parents on the inside covers.

- ***Biff, Chip and Kipper Decode and Develop Stories***
  These new Biff, Chip and Kipper stories have been written to provide language enrichment and help children make the step from phonically regular stories to wider reading. There is support for parents inside every book.

- ***Biff, Chip and Kipper Stories***
  These much-loved stories are ideal for sending home. Support for parents is provided on the inside covers to inspire a love of reading and adventure.

- ***Read with Biff, Chip and Kipper***
  *Read with Biff, Chip and Kipper* is designed to help children learn to read at home. Created by reading experts and based on current teaching practice, the lively stories, humorous illustrations and clear progression will motivate and encourage children to read at home.

  The series consists of *First Stories* and *First Phonics*, which complement the phonic order of the *Floppy's Phonics Sounds and Letters* programme.

  Every book contains hints and tips for parents as well as fun activities and puzzles to help children consolidate their learning.

READ WITH Biff, Chip & Kipper

Dear Parents/Carers,

**Learning to read: supporting your child at home**

Learning to read is one of the most important skills that your child will develop over the next few years. The more support and encouragement that you can offer your child, the more likely it is that he or she will make good progress.

At school we are using the *Oxford Reading Tree* series to take your child through the early stages of learning to read. We are using the *Floppy's Phonics Sounds and Letters* teaching programme, which is a step-by-step phonics reading scheme. It introduces children to the letters and sounds (the alphabetic code) that are at the foundation of all reading and writing.

To reinforce the teaching in school, your child may bring home some books to share with you. These may be:

- *Floppy's Phonics Sounds and Letters Books*, to practise the sounds and letters taught at school
- *Floppy's Phonics Fiction* and *Non-fiction* books to practise reading stories and different text types
- *Biff, Chip and Kipper Stories*, for language development and enrichment.

All the books have notes on the inside cover to guide you on how best to share them with your child.

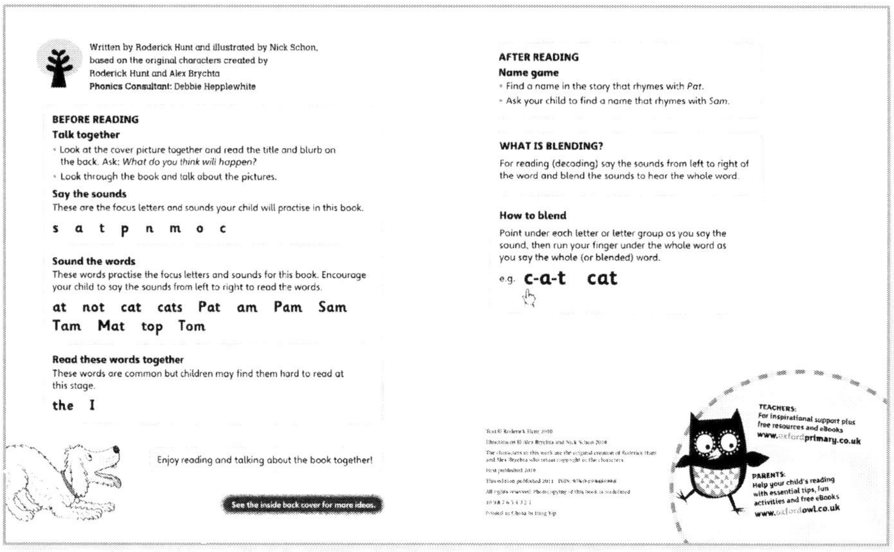
Written by Roderick Hunt and illustrated by Nick Schon, based on the original characters created by Roderick Hunt and Alex Brychta
**Phonics Consultant:** Debbie Hepplewhite

**BEFORE READING**

**Talk together**

- Look at the cover picture together and read the title and blurb on the back. Ask: *What do you think will happen?*
- Look through the book and talk about the pictures.

**Say the sounds**

These are the focus letters and sounds your child will practise in this book.

**s a t p n m o c**

**Sound the words**

These words practise the focus letters and sounds for this book. Encourage your child to say the sounds from left to right to read the words.

**at not cat cats Pat am Pam Sam Tam Mat top Tom**

**Read these words together**

These words are common but children may find them hard to read at this stage.

**the I**

Enjoy reading and talking about the book together!

See the inside back cover for more ideas.

**AFTER READING**

**Name game**

- Find a name in the story that rhymes with *Pat*.
- Ask your child to find a name that rhymes with *Sam*.

**WHAT IS BLENDING?**

For reading (decoding) say the sounds from left to right of the word and blend the sounds to hear the whole word.

**How to blend**

Point under each letter or letter group as you say the sound, then run your finger under the whole word as you say the whole (or blended) word.

e.g. **c-a-t cat**

TEACHERS: For inspirational support plus free resources and eBooks www.oxfordprimary.co.uk

PARENTS: Help your child's reading with essential tips, fun activities and free eBooks www.oxfordowl.co.uk

We may also send home *Grapheme* and *Picture Tiles*, *Activity Sheets* and *Say the Sounds Posters* for your child to practise phonics at home.

You may like to visit www.oxfordowl.co.uk for further information about phonics and helping your child to read, and for free resources and eBooks.

Should you wish to buy any extra books to support your child, you could try the *Read with Biff, Chip and Kipper* series, which have been specially developed to support learning to read at home. This series supports the programme we are using in school.

Best wishes,

# Stage 1 additional activities

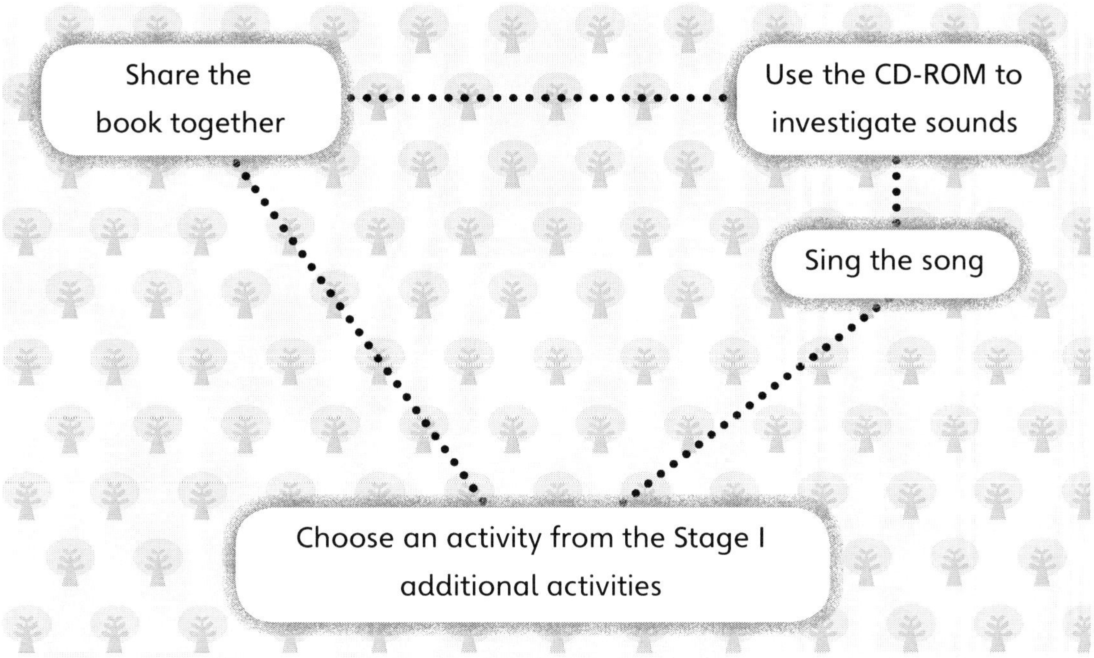


The *Planning, Assessment and Resources* book and CD-ROM provide suggested plans for sharing the Stage I books and investigating the sounds on the Interactive Whiteboard. As suggested in the Stage I plans, the additional activity ideas below can be used as extension activities and to incorporate topics that the children will have come across in the books at Stage I into their planned play activities.

## At Home

**Using different media and mark making**

- Make a collage of garden plants, flowers and insects using collage, paint and other media.
- Ask each child to identify a part of the collage that they would like to label, e.g. the flower's name or the insect's buzzing sound.
- Encourage the children to make meaningful marks on their label.

EYFSP: CLL: Writing 8: begins to form captions

EYFSP: Creative development 3: tries to capture experiences, using a variety of different media

**Making sounds found around the home**

- Remind the children of the mechanical sounds in the book.
- Can the children use instruments (or make their own) to make the sounds of the vacuum cleaner, broom, and lawn mower?
- Encourage them to experiment with shakers, scrapers and everyday objects to make their instruments.
- Can the other children in the group work out which sound they are making?

Letters and Sounds: Aspect 2: instrumental sounds

EYFSP: CLL: Linking sounds and letters I: joins in with rhyming and rhythmic activities

## Out in Town

**Using sounds during play with a small-world town**

- Encourage the children to use the sounds they have explored in the book in their play using their voices and bodies.
- Set up a small world town so the children can play with cars and other vehicles.
- Encourage the children to make train, car and fire engine noises as they play with the toys.

Letters and Sounds: Aspect 3: body percussion

EYFSP: Creative development 6: recognises and explores how sounds can be changed

**Rhymes about the town and transport**

- Use other rhymes about transport and busy towns to learn about rhythm and rhyme.
- Encourage the children to join in with the actions and words of the songs.
  Songs to try:
  The Wheels on the Bus
  Down at the Bus Stop
  Oranges and Lemons
  Girls and Boys Come Out to Play

Letters and Sounds: Aspect 4: rhythm and rhyme

EYFSP: CLL: Linking letters and sounds 2: shows an awareness of rhyme and alliteration

## At the Park

**I-Spy in the park: interactive counting display**

- Use any of the spreads in the book to encourage counting. Ask the children to point out and count the number of dogs, ducks, wheels, runners, skaters etc.
- Tell the children that they are going to make a display called I-Spy in the Park.
- Encourage the children to cut out or draw animals or people inspired by the pictures and write the number that they have cut out or drawn.
- Use the pictures to create an interactive counting display.

EYFSP: CLL: Writing 8: begins to form captions

EYFSP: Creative development 3: tries to capture experiences, using a variety of different media

**Going on a sound walk**

- Go on a sound walk to a local park or around the school playground.
- Collect sounds using a recorder and pictures to use later in class.
- Back in class use the sounds and pictures to retell the walk. Ask the children about which sounds they liked best and make links between the sounds and their experiences.

Letters and Sounds: Aspects 1: environmental sounds

EYFSP: CLL: Language for communication and thinking 5: uses language to imagine and recreate roles and experiences

## Fun at School

**Telling Goldilocks and the Three Bears using instrumental sounds**

- Display the children acting out Goldilocks on the first screen of the CD-ROM.
- Zoom in on the instruments that the children are using and talk about the different sounds that they make.
- Experiment using different instruments and choose an instrument for each of the characters, decide on the beat and volume of each instrument.
- Ask the children to show how they change how they play the instrument to show the bears getting angrier and angrier.
- Add in other instruments to show: opening the door, Goldilocks sitting on the chairs and beds, going up stairs, etc.
- Now tell the story with words and sounds!

Letters and Sounds: Aspects 2: instrumental sounds
EYFSP: Creative development 7: uses imagination in art and design, music, dance, imaginative and role play and stories

**Counting rhymes**

- Use other rhymes about counting to learn about rhythm and rhyme.
- Encourage the children to join in with the actions and words of the songs.

Counting songs:
One, Two, Three, Four, Five, Once I Caught a Fish Alive
This Old Man
One, Two, Buckle My Shoe

Letters and Sounds: Aspect 4: Rhythm and rhyme
EYFSP: CLL: Linking Letters and Sounds 2: shows an awareness of rhyme and alliteration

**Role-play area: Three Bears House**

- Set up a Three Bears House in the role-play area so that the children can act out and tell the story.
- Make masks and/or puppets so that children can tell the story or act it out.

Letters and Sounds: Aspects 3: body percussion
EYFSP: CLL: Language for communication and thinking 5: uses language to imagine and recreate roles and experiences

## At the Farm

**Using sounds during outdoor play/small-world play with a farmyard**

- Encourage the children to use the sounds they have explored in the book in their play using their voices and bodies.
- For example, encourage the children to make plane or tractor noises when they are on scooters and bikes.
- Set up small world play with farm animals and explore the noises that the animals make.
- Visit opportunity: take the children on a visit to a farm to identify the sounds that they can hear.

Letters and Sounds: Aspect 3: body percussion
EYFSP: Creative development 6: recognises and explores how sounds can be changed

**Using instruments to create a storm**

- Remind the children of the big storm in the story.
- Ask the children to think of how they could make the sound of the rain and wind using instruments or by making shakers or wobble boards.
- Work together to build up the sounds from very quiet to very loud, from slow drips to the pitter-patter of a storm!

Letters and Sounds: Aspect 2: instrumental sounds
EYFSP: CLL: Linking sounds and letters 1: joins in with rhyming and rhythmic activities

**Farm and weather rhymes**

- After reading use other rhymes about storms and farms.
- Encourage the children to join in the actions and words of the songs.

Songs to try:
I Hear Thunder
Rain Rain Go Away
The Farmer's In His Den

Letters and Sounds: Aspect 4: rhythm and rhyme
EYFSP: CLL: Linking Letters and Sounds 2: shows an awareness of rhyme and alliteration

## At the Match

**Using chants during play**

- Encourage the children to use the sounds they have explored in the book in their play using their voices and bodies.
- Can they make up clapping rhythms to go with simple chants?
- Can they make the sound of running by running on the spot?
- Encourage the children to use their bodies to make loud and soft noises. Can they work out ways to control the volume of the sounds they make?

Letters and Sounds: Aspect 3: body percussion
EYFSP: Creative development 6: recognises and explores how sounds can be changed

**Looking at sports adverts**

- Bring in a variety of sport programmes, tickets and posters to show the children.
- Discuss how the pictures and words tell you about the different players and what is happening. Show the children the adverts and use the picture clues to work out what they are advertising.
- Use a simple word processing programme to design a poster or programme using pictures for a football match or sports day. Some children may want to add their ideas independently or have an adult help them.

EYFSP: CLL: Writing 6: attempts writing for a variety of purposes, using features of different forms

**Making and finding instruments to form a brass band**

- Remind the children of the big brass band that came on the pitch during half time.
- Look at the pictures in the book (pages 4–5) and ask the children to help you name some of the instruments.
- Collect and make some of the instruments. The children could make their own drums, and trumpets using plastic bottles and tubing, or cones of paper. Encourage them to experiment with the different sounds they can make by blowing in different ways.
- Can the children work together to make a brass band sound?

Letters and Sounds: Aspects 2: instrumental Sounds
EYFSP: Creative development 7: uses imagination in art and design, music, dance, imaginative and role play and stories

# Stage 1+ additional activities

The plans in the *Planning, Assessment and Resources* book and CD-ROM provide a suggested framework for systematically introducing, practising and revising the sounds and graphemes of Stages 1+ to 3. The activity ideas below can be used as creative activities for planned whole class and group play activities, but they should not be used as a substitute for the rigour of the daily core routines of the *Sounds and Letters* programme (see page 28) .

### Make a sound collage linking sounds in words with letters

- Create a wall display using enlarged Grapheme Tiles of focus graphemes with space beneath for children to stick catalogue pictures or their own painted pictures.
- Provide children with catalogues. Ask them to cut out objects which begin with the focus sounds to stick under the correct *Grapheme Tiles*. Add large word labels with the focus grapheme highlighted similar to the labels on the illustrations in the *Sounds and Letters* books: e.g. **k**ite, **c**ot, **t**en**t**.
- For graphemes **ck**, **ll**, **le**, **ss**, provide pre-selected picture examples or ask the children to draw or paint specific pictures, e.g. so**ck**, clo**ck**, du**ck**; dri**ll**, gri**ll**, do**ll**; kett**le**, bott**le**, fidd**le**; dre**ss**, gla**ss**, candy flo**ss**.
- Support children to orally segment all through the words as part of the activity.
- Add to the display as you progress through Stage 1+.

### Match objects to the correct grapheme

- Set up a table with Stage 1+ Grapheme Tiles and a selection of objects – some of which have the same initial, medial or final sound to correspond with the tiles, e.g. pin, dog, duck, rat, rug, pan, hen, pig, bat, cat, kit, kitten, cot, man, band, sock, cup, fan, lid, mug, pen.
- Model how to orally segment the sounds of the object words so that they can be matched to a tile – or use the tiles to spell the words. Support the children as needed.
- Ask the children if they can find two or three further objects in the classroom where the first sound matches with the tiles.
- The children can copy and write the letter shapes while saying the sounds in their personal phonics exercise books. They can also draw the corresponding objects in their books or add to a phonics wall display.

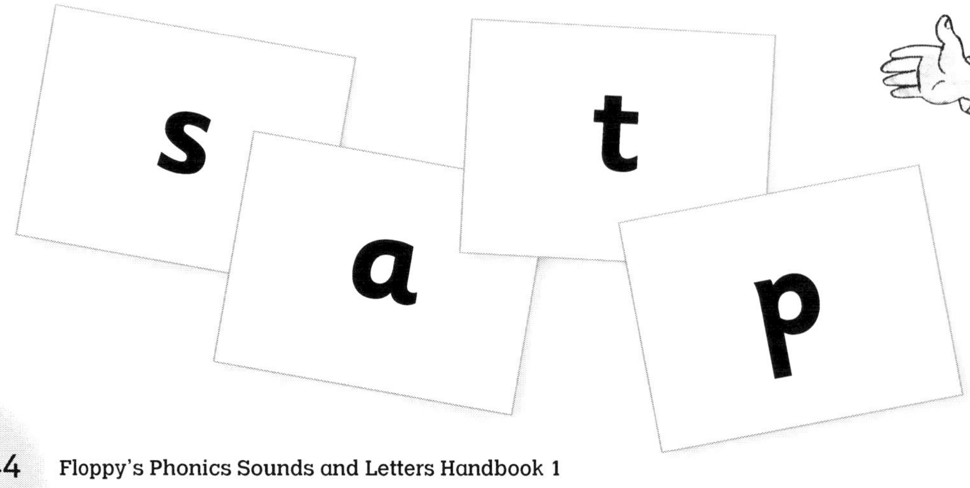

# Stage 2 additional activities

## Printing within letter shapes

- Tape large sheets of paper to table tops or floor, indoors or outdoors.
- Provide paint in trays and a selection of objects for printing which match the letter sound and grapheme taught to date,
  e.g. **s s**ponge; **a a**pple; **t t**oothbrush; **p p**otato and **p**urple **p**aint; **i i**nsect template; **n** piece of **n**et; **m m**agazine page scrunched up; **d d**iamond shape object; **g g**olf ball and **g**reen paint; **o o**range and **o**range paint; **c c**ork; **k k**ey; **ck** so**ck**; **e e**gg box or **e**gg template; **u u**mbrella template; **r r**ag and **r**ed paint; **h h**and print; **b** hair **b**obble with **b**lue paint; **f f**eather; **ff** cu**ff** link; **l l**olly stick; **ll** fri**ll** or she**ll**; **le** bott**le** top; **ss** piece of dre**ss** or template; **j j**am **j**ar lid; **v** piece of **v**el**v**et or **v**est; **w w**ool; **x** candle wa**x** or wa**x** crayon resist; **y y**o-**y**o and **y**ellow paint; **z z**ip; **zz** pu**zz**le piece; **qu qu**ilt stuffing; **ch ch**ain print or **ch**alk pattern; **sh sh**oe (doll's); **th th**umb and/or **th**imble; **ng** ri**ng** and/or stri**ng**; **dge** ba**dge**; **ve** glo**ve**; **wh wh**eel; **cks** clo**cks** template (maths resource); **tch** eye pa**tch**; **nk** han**k**ie and pi**nk** paint or pi**nk** i**nk** felt pens.
- Draw large hollow letter shapes and encourage the children to print in the direction that letters are written.
- Cut out the letter shapes, make a display and refer to it for the children to say the sounds and air-write the letter shapes.

## Muddle the grapheme lozenges and say the sounds

- Photocopy several copies of the Stage 1+ and Stage 2 *Say the Sounds Poster*. Laminate if you want to make a permanent game.
- Cut out the grapheme lozenges. Select the graphemes that the children have been learning to date. Place the lozenges face downwards and muddle them up.
- The children take it in turns to turn over a lozenge and 'say the sounds'. If they get all the sounds on a lozenge correct, they score a point.
- Replace the lozenges face downwards to continue the game. Muddle the lozenges.
- Further, the children can use coloured crayons to practise writing the letter shapes of a grapheme lozenge as a repeated pattern. Encourage the children to say the sounds whilst writing the letter shapes.
- Alternatively, the children can stick paper lozenges into their exercise books as a permanent prompt to say the sounds and write the letter shapes.

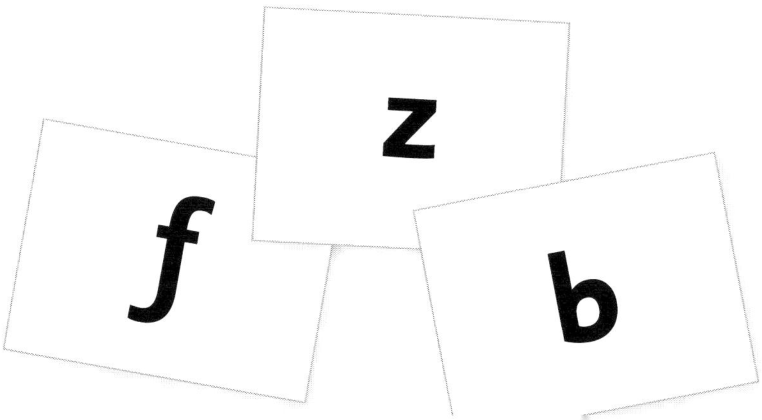

# Stage 3 additional activities

### Painting poem pictures

- Write the poem from the end of the *Sounds and Letters* book that you have been working with onto a large sheet of paper and display it next to the painting area.
- Together, read the poem through a few times adding expression as appropriate.
- Discuss the meaning of any new words and the type of poem it is, e.g. a nonsense poem.
- The children can paint a picture to represent the poem or parts of the poem.
- Work with the children to label different words in the picture with the focus sounds.
- Display the pictures with the poem. The children can re-read the poem at any time increasing their fluency and expression.

### Story-telling

- Display a spread from the CD-ROM on the interactive whiteboard. Select the audio buttons to listen for the focus sounds in the spoken words.
- Ask children to draw their own version of the picture adding a couple of new features with the focus sound. They can practise orally segmenting words in their picture. Remind them to say the words slowly and tally the sounds on thumb and fingers of their left hand, palm facing.
- Support the children to label some of the objects, characters and actions in their pictures using *The Alphabet Poster* and displayed Say the Sounds Posters for grapheme prompts. Display some or all of the pictures.
- Further, the children can sit in pairs to tell the story of their picture and then sit in a class circle for some to repeat their story and ask questions of one another.

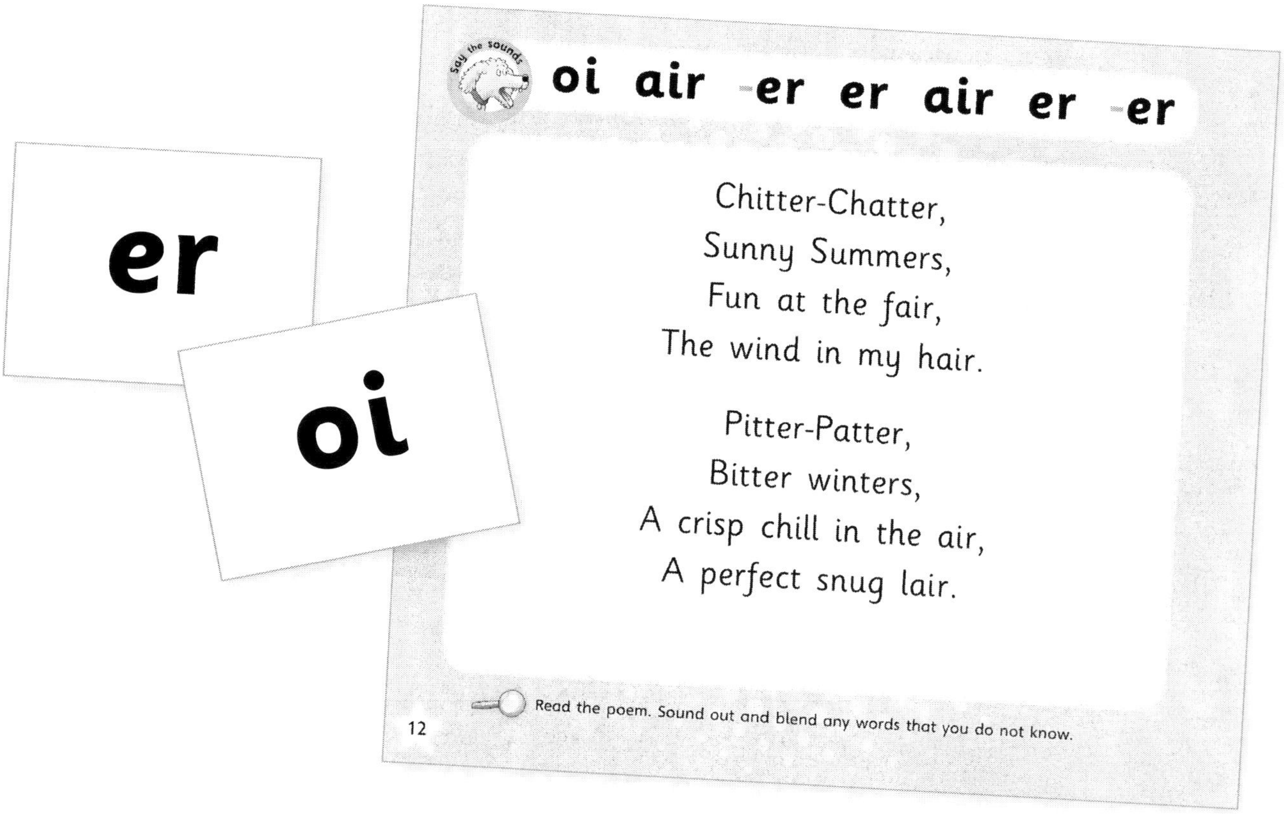

# Say the sounds

**Oxford Reading Tree Sounds and Letters Stage 1+**

| | | | |
|---|---|---|---|
| s | a | t | p |
| i | n | m | d |
| g | o | c | k |
| -ck | e | u | r |
| h | b | f | -ff |
| l | -ll | -le | -ss |

# Say the sounds

## Oxford Reading Tree Sounds and Letters Stage 2

| | | | |
|---|---|---|---|
| j | v | | w |
| -x | y | | z |
| -zz | qu | | ch |
| sh | th | th | -ng |
| -dge | -ve | | wh |
| -cks | -tch | | -nk |

# Say the sounds

## Oxford Reading Tree Sounds and Letters Stage 3

ai ee -y -igh -y

oa -oo oo

ar or ur

ow oi ear

air er -er

-ue -ue -ure -ture

# Say the sounds

## Oxford Reading Tree Sounds and Letters Stage 1+

| | | | |
|---|---|---|---|
| e | f | u | m |
| c | -ss | | b |
| -le | k | d | n |
| -ll | a | h | l |
| r | -ff | p | g |
| s | -ck | t | i |

# Say the sounds

## Oxford Reading Tree Sounds and Letters Stage 2

| | | | |
|---|---|---|---|
| y | sh | | w |
| -zz | -x | | th |
| th | ch | j | qu |
| -ng | | v | z |
| -nk | wh | | -dge |
| -tch | -cks | | -ve |

# Say the sounds

## Oxford Reading Tree Sounds and Letters Stage 3

| | | | |
|---|---|---|---|
| or | ur | oi | ear |
| ow | ai | air | |
| ee | -igh | -y | |
| -y | -oo | oo | |
| -ue | -ue | oa | er |
| -er | -ture | -ure | |

**Name** ..........................................................  **Date** ..........................................................

s

Say the sound. Trace the letter.

Say the word. Listen for the /s/ sound.

s  s  s s  s s s

 s  s s  s s  s

Point and say the sound.

s s s s

Say the sound. Trace the letters. Write the letters.

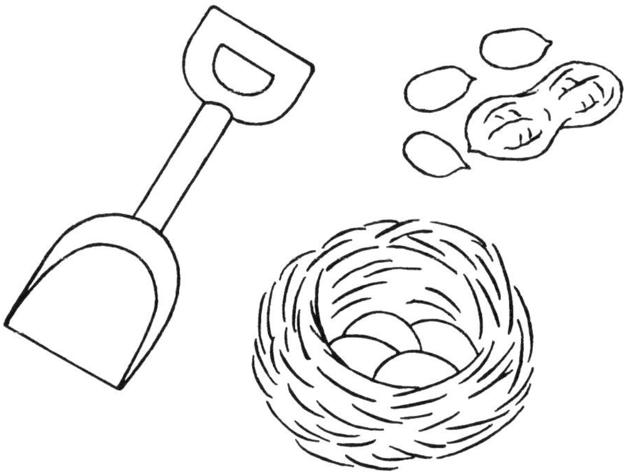

Say the words. Can you hear the /s/ sound?

Draw something beginning with **s**.

s

**Name** ................................................................ **Date** ........................................................

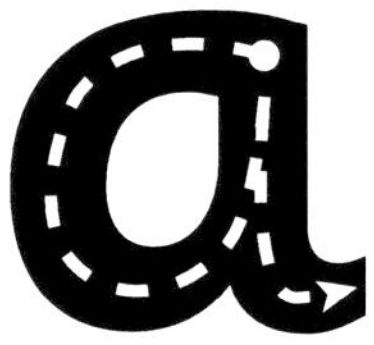

Say the sound. Trace the letter.

Say the word. Listen for the /a/ sound.

a  a  a a  a a

 a  a a  a a a

Point and say the sound.

Say the sound. Trace the letters. Write the letters.

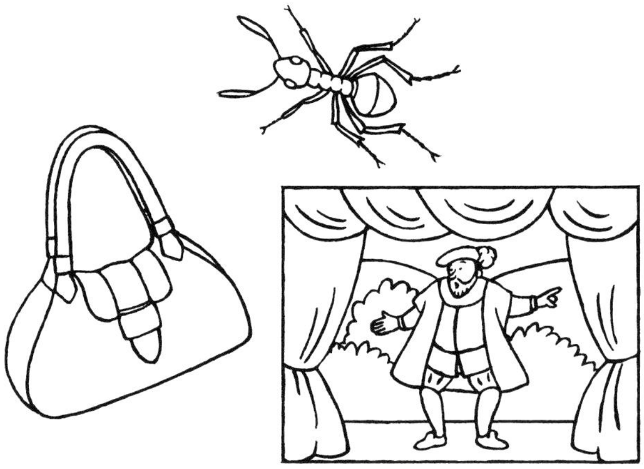

Say the words. Can you hear the /a/ sound?

Draw something beginning with **a**.

s **a**

**Name** ..............................................................  **Date** ......................................................

t

Say the sound. Trace the letter.

Say the word. Listen for the /t/ sound.

t a t t s t a t s

at sat at tat sat at

Point and say the sounds. Blend to read the words.

t t t t

Say the sound. Trace the letters. Write the letters.

Say the words. Can you hear the /t/ sound?

Draw something beginning with **t**.

Say the sounds

s a t

**Name** ..............................................................  **Date** ........................................................

p

Say the sound. Trace the letter.

Say the word. Listen for the /p/ sound.

p t s a t p s a p

sat pat tap pat taps

Point and say the sounds. Blend to read the words.

p p p p

Say the sound. Trace the letters. Write the letters.

Say the words. Can you hear the /p/ sound?

Draw something beginning with **p**.

s a t **p**

**Name** ............................................................ **Date** ............................................................

i

Say the sound. Trace the letter.

Say the word. Listen for the /i/ sound.

i s p i a t i s p t

it sat is tip sat it is

its pit pip sip its pip

Point and say the sounds. Blend to read the words.

i i i i

Say the sound. Trace the letters. Write the letters.

Say the words. Can you hear the /i/ sound?

Draw something beginning with **i**.

s a t p **i**

**Name** ..............................................................  **Date** ..............................................................

# n

Say the sound. Trace the letter.

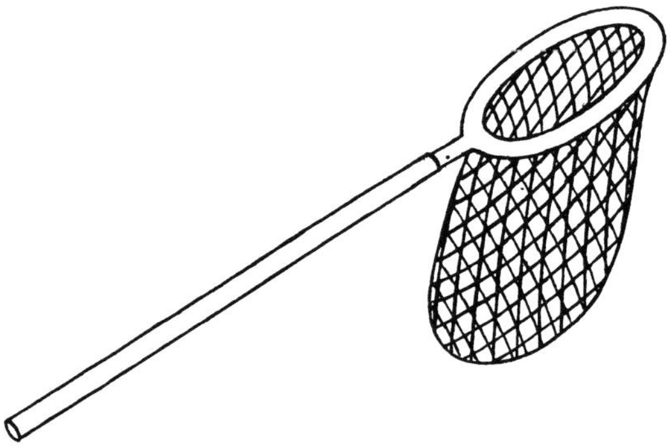

Say the word. Listen for the /n/ sound.

n s i a p t n s i

an nip it at nip an

nap pin pan ant pin

Point and say the sounds. Blend to read the words.

n n n n

Say the sound. Trace the letters. Write the letters.

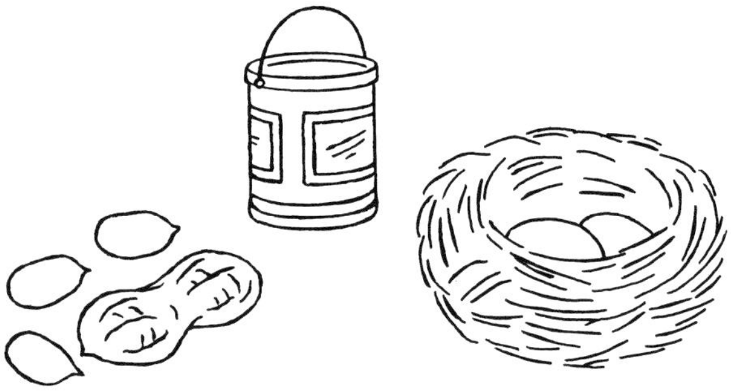

Say the words. Can you hear the /n/ sound?

Draw something beginning with **n**.

Say the sounds

s a t p i **n**

**Name** ..........................................................................  **Date** ..........................................................................

m

Say the sound. Trace the letter.

Say the word. Listen for the /m/ sound.

m a t m p n i s p

map mat sit tan Pam

man nip maps mint

Point and say the sounds. Blend to read the words.

m m m m

Say the sound. Trace the letters. Write the letters.

Say the words. Can you hear the /m/ sound?

Draw something beginning with **m**.

s a t p i n **m**

**Name** ..................................................................... **Date** ......................................................

d

Say the sound. Trace the letter.

Say the word. Listen for the /d/ sound.

d m n p a d t s d

dip dap sad mad dad

and dips sand damp

Point and say the sounds. Blend to read the words.

d d d d

Say the sound. Trace the letters. Write the letters.

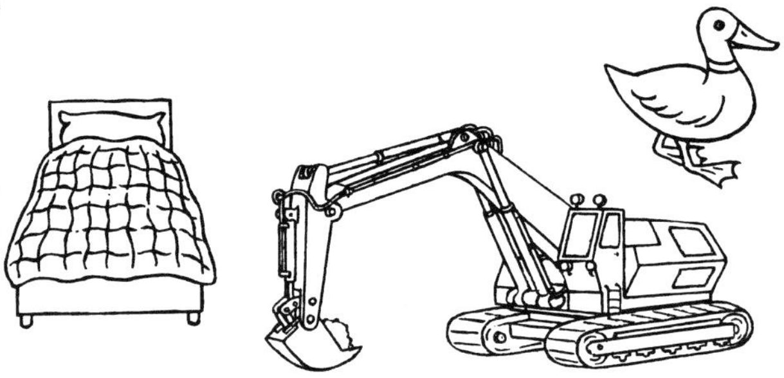

Say the words. Can you hear the /d/ sound?

Draw something beginning with **d**.

Say the sounds

s a t p i n m **d**

**Name** ..............................................................  **Date** ..............................................................

g

Say the sound. Trace the letter.

Say the word. Listen for the /g/ sound.

g s m p a g d g t

dig gas man gap dig

nag sag gaps nags

Point and say the sounds. Blend to read the words.

g g g g

Say the sound. Trace the letters. Write the letters.

Say the words. Can you hear the /g/ sound?

Draw something beginning with **g**.

Say the sounds

s a t p i n m d **g**

**Name** ..............................................................  **Date** ..............................................................

o

Say the sound. Trace the letter.

Say the word. Listen for the /o/ sound.

o m d g s a o n o

pot dog got it dot on

and dots spot pond

Point and say the sounds. Blend to read the words.

o o o o

Say the sound. Trace the letters. Write the letters.

Say the words. Can you hear the /o/ sound?

Draw something beginning with **o**.

Say the sounds

s a t p i n m d g **o**

**Name** ..............................................................................  **Date** ...........................................................................

c

Say the sound. Trace the letter.

Say the word. Listen for the /k/ sound.

c g m p c i t n c

cap cot can cat act

cats camp cost picnic

Point and say the sounds. Blend to read the words.

c c c c

Say the sound. Trace the letters. Write the letters.

Say the words. Can you hear the /k/ sound?

Draw something beginning with **c**.

Say the sounds

a t p i n m d g o **c**

**Name** ..............................................................  **Date** ..............................................................

k

Say the sound. Trace the letter.

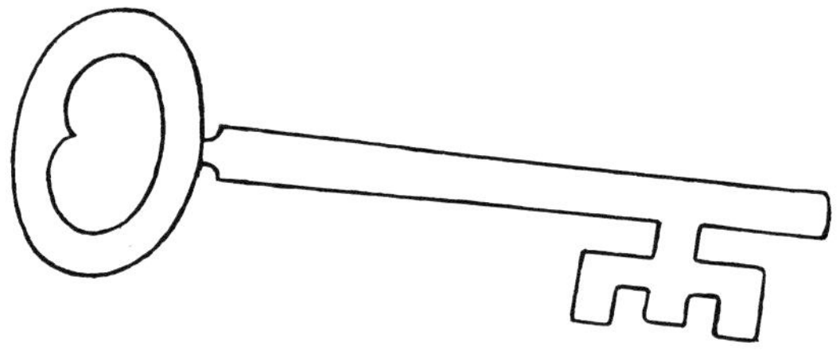

Say the word. Listen for the /k/ sound.

kit at dad sit kit cap

kiss man nod kid kiss

cats skip kids skin skip

Blend to read the words.

k k k k

Say the sound. Trace the letters. Write the letters.

Say the words. Can you hear the /k/ sound?

Draw something beginning with **k**.

Say the sounds

t p i n m d g o c **k**

**Name** ..............................................................  **Date** ..........................................................

ck

Say the sound. Trace the letters.

Say the word. Listen for the /k/ sound.

sack pick pack kick

tick-tock sock packs

snack stack sticks stock

Blend to read the words.

ck ck ck

Say the sound. Trace the letters. Write the letters.

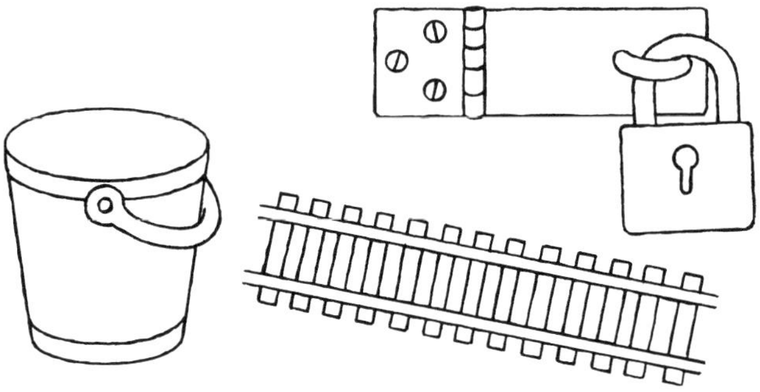

Say the words. Can you hear the /k/ sound?

Draw something ending in **ck**.

p i n m d g o c k **-ck**

**Name** ..........................................................................  **Date** ..........................................................................

# e

Say the sound. Trace the letter.

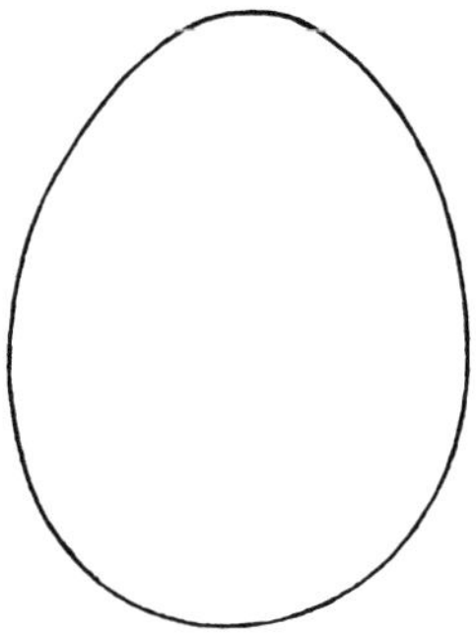

Say the word. Listen for the /e/ sound.

## men net pen net den

## peg get neck peck get

## deck pets sent mend

Blend to read the words.

## e e e e

Say the sound. Trace the letters. Write the letters.

Say the words. Can you hear the /e/ sound?

Draw something beginning with **e**.

Say the sounds

i n m d g o c k -ck **e**

**Name** ..........................................................................  **Date** ..........................................................................

u

Say the sound. Trace the letter.

Say the word. Listen for the /u/ sound.

up tug cup sun cut

dug mud duck luck

must dump pump stuck

Blend to read the words.

u u u u

Say the sound. Trace the letters. Write the letters.

Say the words. When can you hear the /u/ sound?

Draw something beginning with **u**.

Say the sounds

m d g o c k -ck e **u**

**Name** ............................................................ **Date** ............................................................

r

Say the sound. Trace the letter.

Say the word. Listen for the /r/ sound.

# run rug red rip rod
# rock rats drop rest
# dress crack drumstick

Blend to read the words.

r r r r

Say the sound. Trace the letters. Write the letters.

Say the words. Can you hear the /r/ sound?

Draw something beginning with **r**.

Say the sounds

m d g o c k -ck e u **r**

**Name** ..............................................................  **Date** ..............................................................

h

Say the sound. Trace the letter.

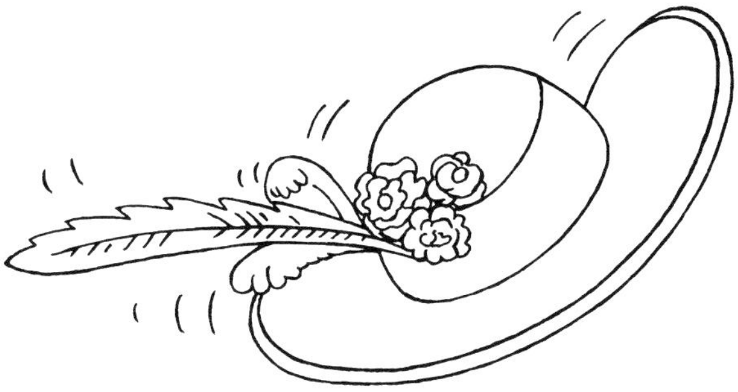

Say the word. Listen for the /h/ sound.

hot hen hot had hen

hops hiss hop ham

hand hunt hump hidden

Blend to read the words.

h h h h

Say the sound. Trace the letters. Write the letters.

Say the words. Can you hear the /h/ sound?

Draw something beginning with **h**.

d g o c k -ck e u r **h**

**Name** ................................................................ **Date** ........................................................

# b

Say the sound. Trace the letter.

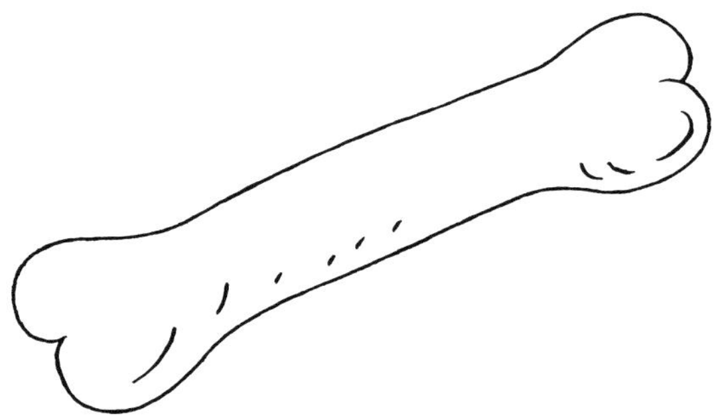

Say the word. Listen for the /b/ sound.

big bun bed bag back

bits bobs bats bend

bump crab bump rabbit

Blend to read the words.

b b b b

Say the sound. Trace the letters. Write the letters.

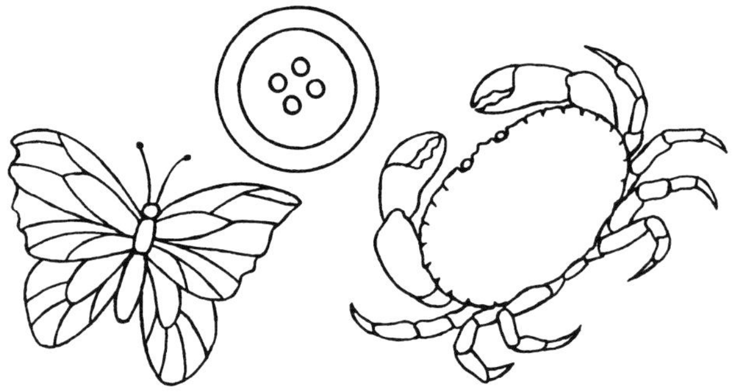

Say the words. Can you hear the /b/ sound?

Draw something beginning with **b**.

Say the sounds

g o c k -ck e u r h **b**

**Name** ..................................................................... **Date** ...........................................................

Say the sound. Trace the letter.

Say the word. Listen for the /f/ sound.

fin fun fog fed fat

if fan fist frog soft

fast facts draft of

Blend to read the words.

f f f f

Say the sound. Trace the letters. Write the letters.

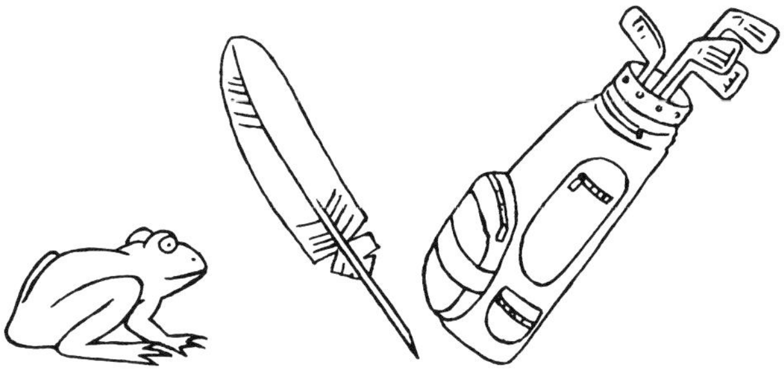

Say the words. Can you hear the /f/ sound?

Draw something beginning with **f**.

Say the sounds

o c k -ck e u r h b f

**Name** ..........................................................................   **Date** ..........................................................................

ff

Say the sound. Trace the letters.

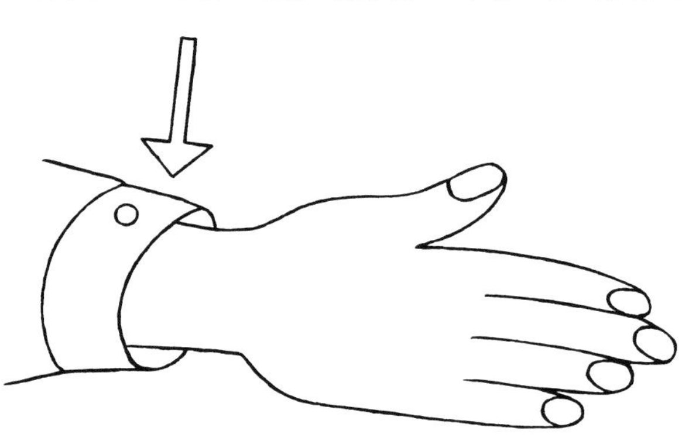

Say the word. Listen for the /f/ sound.

off huff puff cuff tiff

stuff scuff fluff puffin

Blend to read the words.

ff ff ff

Say the sound. Trace the letters. Write the letters.

Say the words. Can you hear the /f/ sound?

Draw something ending in **ff**.

Say the sounds

c k -ck e u r h b f -ff

**Name** ..................................................................... **Date** .....................................................................

l

Say the sound. Trace the letter.

Say the word. Listen for the /l/ sound.

led lag let lock leg

lick slips lips list a lot

luck club slug cluck

Blend to read the words.

l l l l

Say the sound. Trace the letters. Write the letters.

Say the words. Can you hear the /l/ sound?

Draw something beginning with **l**.

Say the sounds

k -ck e u r h b f -ff **l**

**Name** ..................................................... **Date** .....................................................

ll

Say the sound. Trace the letters.

Say the word. Listen for the /l/ sound.

ill tell bill doll fill sell
full bell gull hull hills
drill skull lollipop frills

Blend to read the words.

ll ll ll

Say the sound. Trace the letters. Write the letters.

Say the words. Can you hear the /l/ sound?

Draw something ending in **ll**.

-ck e u r h b f -ff l **-ll**

**Name** ..............................................................

**Date** ..............................................................

**le**

Say the sound. Trace the letters.

Say the word. Listen for the /ul/ sound.

little kettle middle

tickle rattle puddle

tackle muddle trickle

Blend to read the words.

**le** le le

Say the sound. Trace the letters. Write the letters.

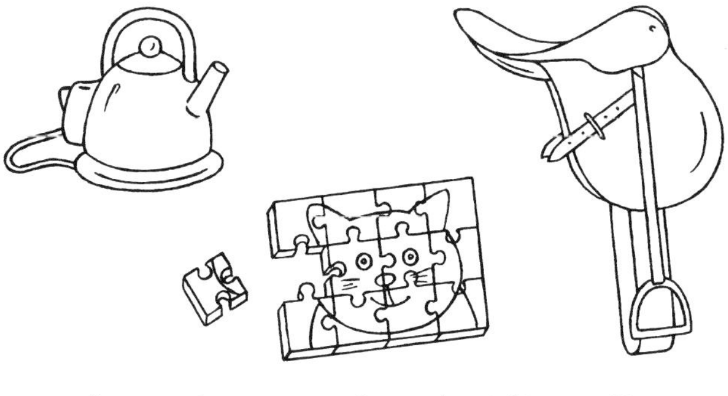

Say the words. Can you hear the /ul/ sound?

Draw something ending in **le**.

Say the sounds

e u r h b f -ff l -ll **-le**

**Name** ..............................................................  **Date** ..............................................................

**ss**

Say the sound. Trace the letters.

Say the word. Listen for the /s/ sound.

mess boss miss less

hiss mess kiss moss

puss press cress bless

Blend to read the words.

**ss** ss ss

Say the sound. Trace the letters. Write the letters.

Say the words. Can you hear the /s/ sound?

Draw something ending in **ss**.

Say the sounds

r h b f -ff l -ll -le **-ss**

**Name** ..................................................................... **Date** .....................................................................

j

Say the sound. Trace the letter.

Say the word. Listen for the /j/ sound.

jug jet jam jig jab jog

Jill Jack just jump jets

jacket juggle jet lag just

Blend to read the words.

j j j j

Say the sound. Trace the letters. Write the letters.

Say the words. Can you hear the /j/ sound?

Draw something beginning with **j**.

Say the sounds

h b f -ff l -ll -le -ss j

**Name** ..............................................................  **Date** ..............................................

v

Say the sound. Trace the letter.

Say the word. Listen for the /v/ sound.

vet van Vic vest Val van

vast vent vans vets vest

visit Kevin velvet invent

Blend to read the words.

v v v v

Say the sound. Trace the letters. Write the letters.

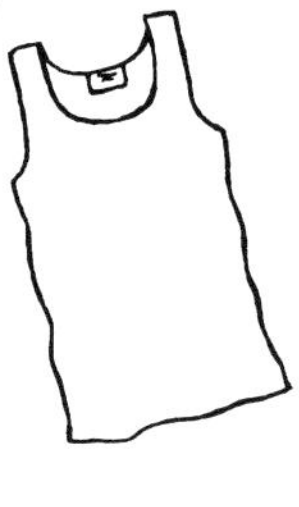

Say the words. Can you hear the /v/ sound?

Draw something beginning with **v**.

Say the sounds

b f -ff l -ll -le -ss j **v**

**Name** ..............................................................  **Date** ..............................................................

w

Say the sound. Trace the letter.

Say the word. Listen for the /w/ sound.

win wag web will win

wet well went wags webs

west swim wiggle cobweb

Blend to read the words.

w w w

Say the sound. Trace the letters. Write the letters.

Say the words. Can you hear the /w/ sound?

Draw something beginning with **w**.

f -ff l -ll -le -ss j v **w**

**Name** ..............................................................  **Date** ..............................................................

x

Say the sound. Trace the letter.

Say the word. Listen for the /ks/ sound.

fix ox wax box tax fix

six Max mix fox six oxen

foxes text relax next text

Blend to read the words.

x x x x

Say the sound. Trace the letters. Write the letters.

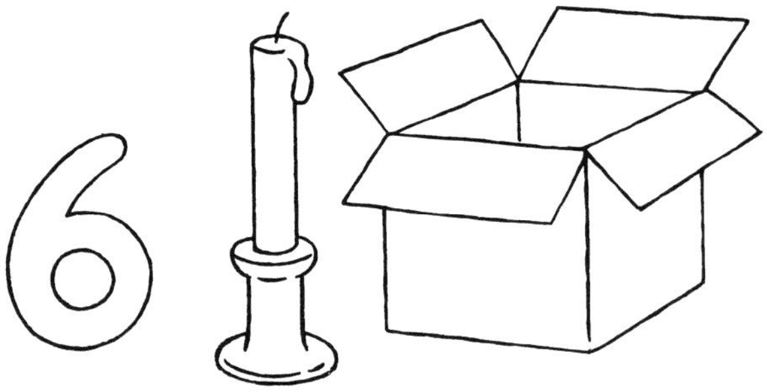

Say the words. Can you hear the /ks/ sound?

Draw something ending in **x**.

Say the sounds

-ff l -ll -le -ss j v w -**x**

**Name** ..........................................................  **Date** ..........................................................

y

Say the sound. Trace the letter.

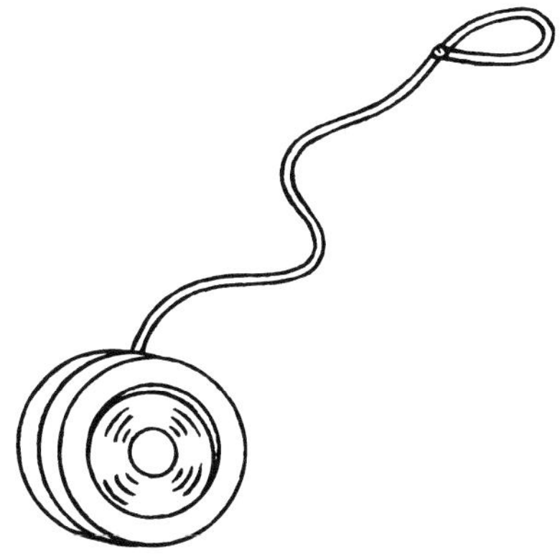

Say the word. Listen for the /y/ sound.

yes yap yet yell yes yet

yak yells yelp yaps yuck

just vest wobble Yasmin

Blend to read the words.

y y y y

Say the sound. Trace the letters. Write the letters.

Say the words. Can you hear the /y/ sound?

Draw something beginning with **y**.

l -ll -le -ss j v w -x **y**

**Name** ..........................................................................   **Date** ..................................................................

z

Say the sound. Trace the letter.

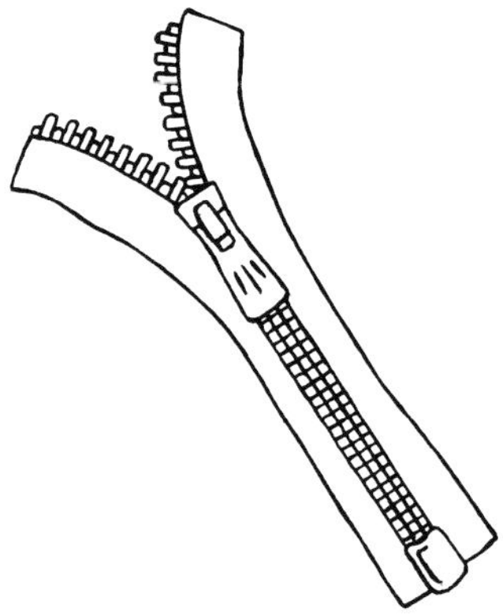

Say the word. Listen for the /z/ sound.

zip zap zed zip zap zed

zig zag vet zips zaps yaps

zest zebra Zak zest zebra

Blend to read the words.

z z z z

Say the sound. Trace the letters. Write the letters.

Say the words. Can you hear the /z/ sound?

Draw something beginning with **z**.

Say the sounds

-ll -le -ss j v w -x y **z**

**Name** ..............................................................   **Date** ..............................................................

zz

Say the sound. Trace the letters.

Say the word. Listen for the /z/ sound.

buzz fizz jazz fuzz buzz

puzzle fizzle muzzle fizz

razzle-dazzle drizzle grizzle

Blend to read the words.

zz zz zz

Say the sound. Trace the letters. Write the letters.

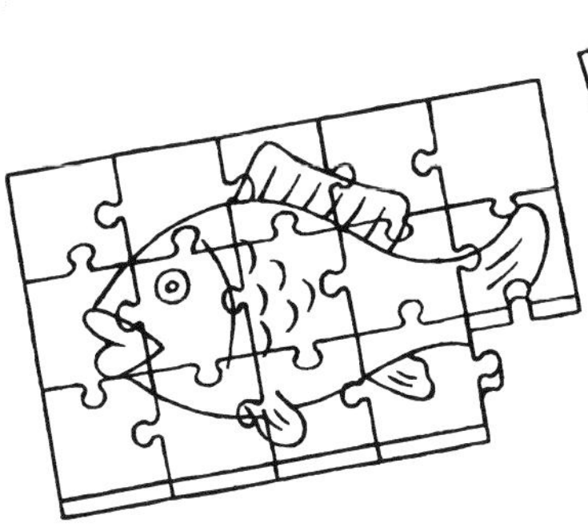

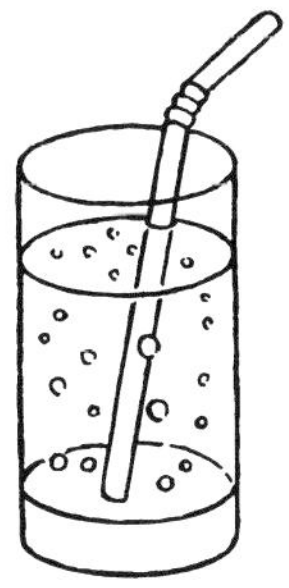

Say the words. Can you hear the /z/ sound?

Draw something ending with **zz**.

-le -ss j v w -x y z **-zz**

**Name** ....................................................................... **Date** .......................................................................

# qu

Say the sound. Trace the letters.

Say the word. Listen for the /kw/ sound.

quick quit quack quest

quilt quins queen squid

squint liquid squirrel

Blend to read the words.

qu qu qu

Say the sound. Trace the letters. Write the letters.

Say the words. Can you hear the /kw/ sound?

Draw something beginning with **qu**.

Say the sounds

-ss j v w -x y z -zz **qu**

**Name** ......................................................................... **Date** ..............................................................

# ch

Say the sound. Trace the letters.

Say the word. Listen for the /ch/ sound.

chat chin chick much

chips rich chop chill chess

check lunch munch squelch

Blend to read the words.

ch ch ch

Say the sound. Trace the letters. Write the letters.

Say the words. Can you hear the /ch/ sound?

Draw something beginning with **ch**.

Say the sounds

j v w -x y z -zz qu **ch**

**Name** ..................................................................... **Date** ......................................................

sh

Say the sound. Trace the letters.

Say the word. Listen for the /sh/ sound.

shop shed shut fish ship

shall dish shells shock

wish hush shop brush

Blend to read the words.

sh sh sh

Say the sound. Trace the letters. Write the letters.

Say the words. Can you hear the /sh/ sound?

Draw something beginning with **sh**.

w -x y z -zz qu ch **sh**

**Name** ..............................................................

**Date** ..............................................................

th

Say the sound. Trace the letters.

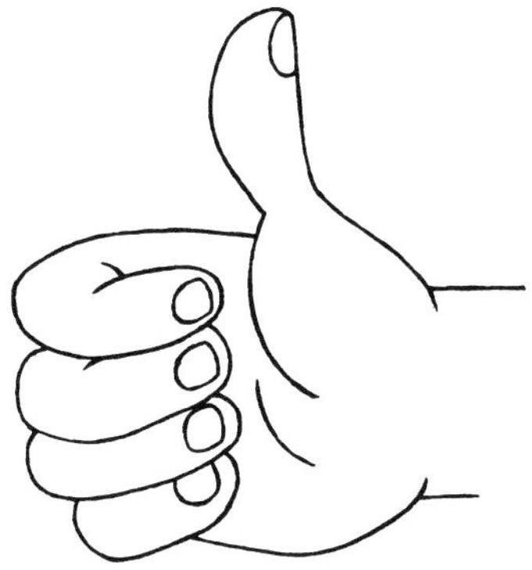

Say the word. Listen for the /th/ sounds.

thin thick moth maths

the with this that then

then them thrush thrill

Blend to read the words.

th th th

Say the sound. Trace the letters. Write the letters.

Say the words. Can you hear the /th/ sound?

Draw something ending in **th**.

Say the sounds

-x y z -zz qu ch sh **th**

**Name** ..........................................................................  **Date** ..................................................................

# ng

Say the sound. Trace the letters.

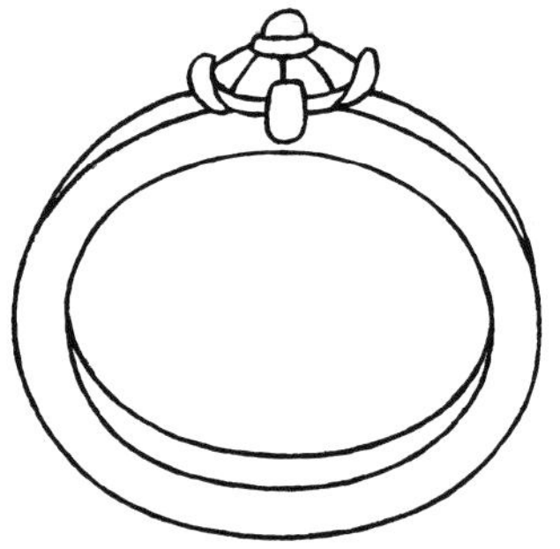

Say the word. Listen for the /ng/ sound.

song bang wing long

hang thing gong rings

swing lungs bring ping-pong

Blend to read the words.

ng ng ng

Say the sound. Trace the letters. Write the letters.

Say the words. Can you hear the /ng/ sound?

Draw something ending in **ng**.

Say the sounds

z -zz qu ch sh th **-ng**

**Name** ................................................................ **Date** ........................................................

dge

Say the sound. Trace the letters.

Say the word. Listen for the /j/ sound.

jam jug jet just jump jog

hedge badge judge edge

sludge midges fridge bridge

Blend to read the words. Some words revise **j** and other words practise **dge**.

dge dge

Say the sound. Trace the letters. Write the letters.

Say the words. Can you hear the /j/ sound?

Draw something ending in **dge**.

-zz qu ch sh th -ng **-dge**

**Name** ..................................................................... **Date** ......................................................

# ve

Say the sound. Trace the letters.

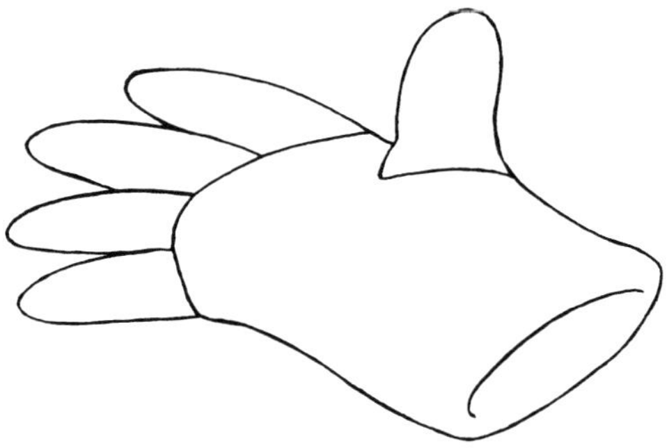

Say the word. Listen for the /v/ sound.

van vet vest invent Vic

have give live love gives

dove above gloves doves

Blend to read the words. Some words revise **v** and other words practise **ve**.

ve ve ve

Say the sound. Trace the letters. Write the letters.

Say the words. Can you hear the /v/ sound?

Draw something ending in **ve**.

qu ch sh th -ng -dge -**ve**

**Name** ..............................................................  **Date** ..............................................................

wh

Say the sound. Trace the letters.

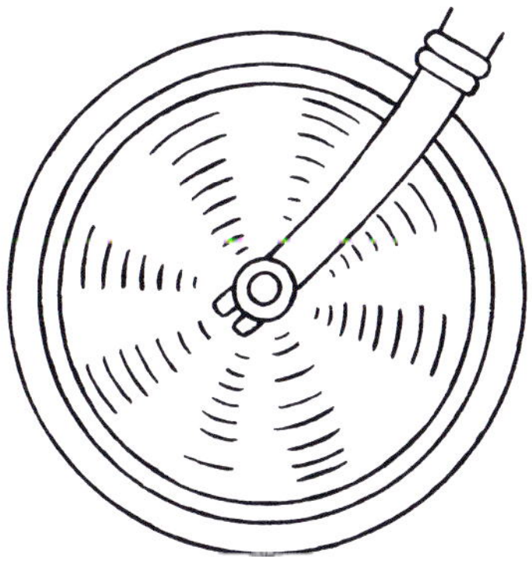

Say the word. Listen for the /w/ sound.

wet win will went wig

well west wagon wobble

when whisk whip whizz

Blend to read the words. Some words revise **w** and other words practise **wh**.

wh wh

Say the sound. Trace the letters. Write the letters.

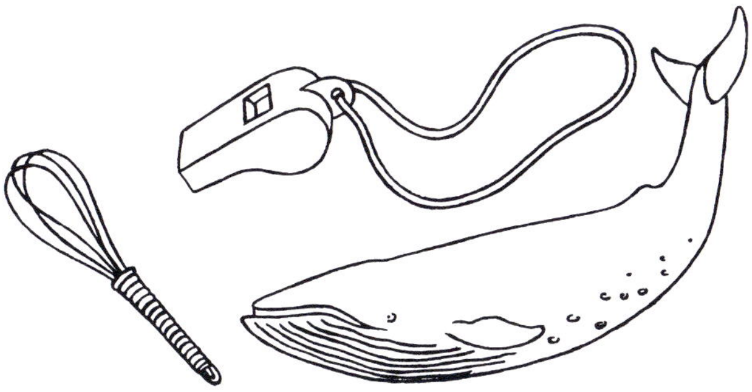

Say the words. Can you hear the /w/ sound?

Draw something beginning with **wh**.

Say the sounds

sh th -ng -dge -ve **wh**

**Name** ..........................................................................  **Date** ..........................................................................

# cks

Say the sound. Trace the letters.

Say the word. Listen for the /ks/ sound.

six box wax mix fix tax

ox fox rocks packs licks

socks picks sticks bricks

Blend to read the words. Some words revise **x** and other words practise **cks**.

cks cks

Say the sound. Trace the letters. Write the letters.

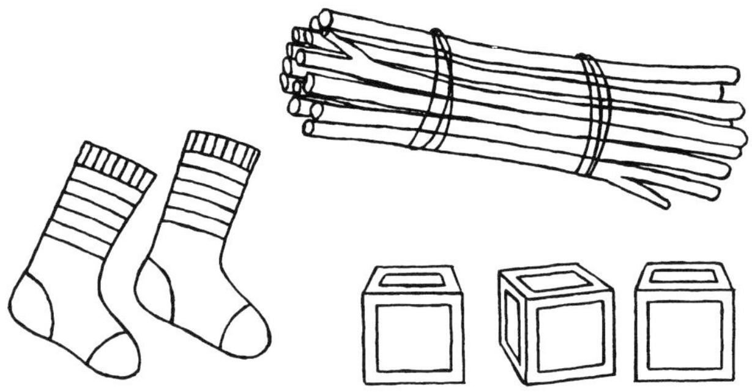

Say the words. Can you hear the /ks/ sound?

Draw something ending in **cks**.

th -ng -dge -ve wh -cks

**Name** ..................................................... **Date** .....................................................

tch

Say the sound. Trace the letters.

Say the word. Listen for the /ch/ sound.

chess chap chimp chug

pinch punch squelch catch

patch hutch fetch match

Blend to read the words. Some words revise **ch** and other words practise **tch**.

tch tch

Say the sound. Trace the letters. Write the letters.

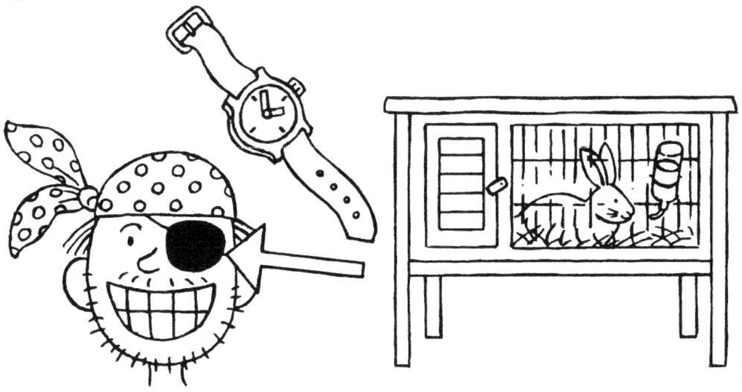

Say the words. Can you hear the /ch/ sound?

Draw something ending in **tch**.

Say the sounds

-dge -ve wh -cks **-tch**

**Name** ............................................................ **Date** ............................................................

nk

Say the sound. Trace the letters.

Say the word. Listen for the /ngk/ sound.

sing pong king sting wing

pink bank wink sink blink

think thank drink blanket

Blend to read the words. Some words revise **ng** and other words practise **nk**.

nk nk nk

Say the sound. Trace the letters. Write the letters.

Say the words. Can you hear the /ngk/ sound?

Draw something ending in **nk**.

Say the sounds

-dge -ve wh -cks -tch -**nk**

**Name** ..............................................................................   **Date** ..............................................................

ai

Say the sound. Trace the letters.

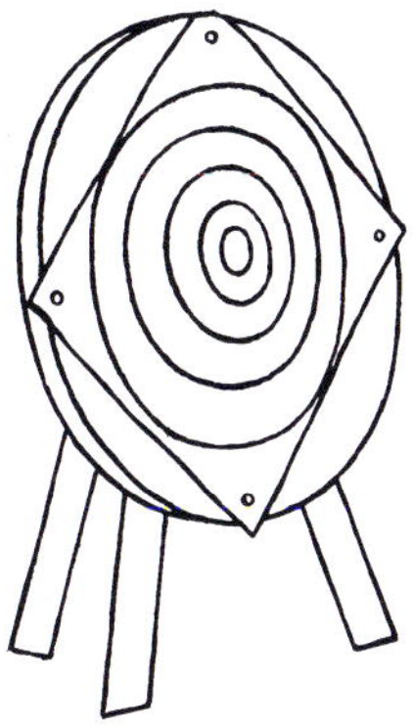

Say the word. Listen for the /ai/ sound.

aim   aid   rain   tail   maid

paid   sail   wait   pain   nails

snail   trail   train   paint

Blend to read the words.

ai   ai

Say the sound. Trace the letters. Write the letters.

Say the words. Can you hear the /ai/ sound?

Draw something with the /ai/ sound (**ai**) in it.

-ve   wh   -cks   -tch   -nk   **ai**

**Name** ..............................................................  **Date** ..............................................................

**ee**

Say the sound. Trace the letters.

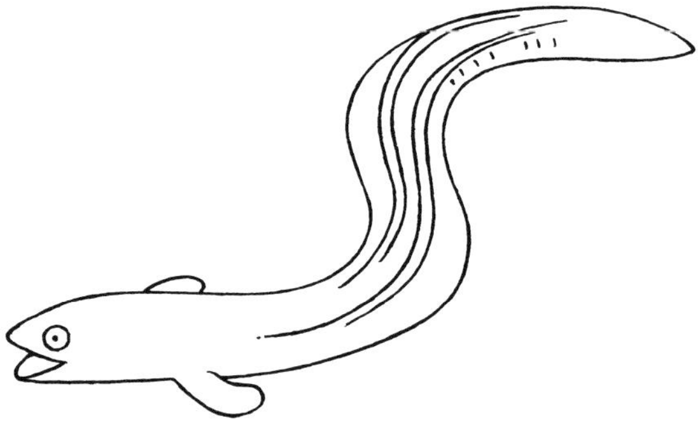

Say the word. Listen for the /ee/ sound.

bee see eel feel seeds

meet feet deep sweet bees

teeth green tree free street

Blend to read the words.

**ee** ee

Say the sound. Trace the letters. Write the letters.

Say the words. Can you hear the /ee/ sound?

Draw something with the /ee/ sound (**ee**) in it.

Say the sounds

wh -cks -tch -nk ai **ee**

**Name** ........................................................................ **Date** ......................................................

# igh

Say the sound. Trace the letters.

Say the word. Listen for the /igh/ sound.

high sigh light night tight

thigh sight fight tights

might fright frighten bright

Blend to read the words.

igh igh

Say the sound. Trace the letters. Write the letters.

Say the words. Can you hear the /igh/ sound?

Draw something with the /igh/ sound (**igh**) in it.

Say the sounds

-cks -tch -nk ai ee **-igh**

**Name** ..............................................................................  **Date** ..............................................................................

# oa

Say the sound. Trace the letters.

Say the word. Listen for the /oa/ sound.

coat road soap goal toad

loaf moan soak boat oak

croak foal toast float goat

Blend to read the words.

oa oa

Say the sound. Trace the letters. Write the letters.

Say the words. Can you hear the /oa/ sound?

Draw something with the /oa/ sound (**oa**) in it.

Say the sounds

-tch -nk ai ee -igh **oa**

**Name** ........................................................................ **Date** ..................................................................

oo

Say the sound. Trace the letters.

Say the word. Listen for the short /oo/ sound.

book good cook look

hood hook shook took

wool wood wooden

Blend to read the words.

oo oo

Say the sound. Trace the letters. Write the letters.

Say the words. Can you hear the short /oo/ sound?

Draw something with the short /oo/ sound (**oo**) in it.

-nk ai ee -igh oa -**oo**

**Name** ..................................................................... **Date** ..........................................................

# oo

Say the sound. Trace the letters.

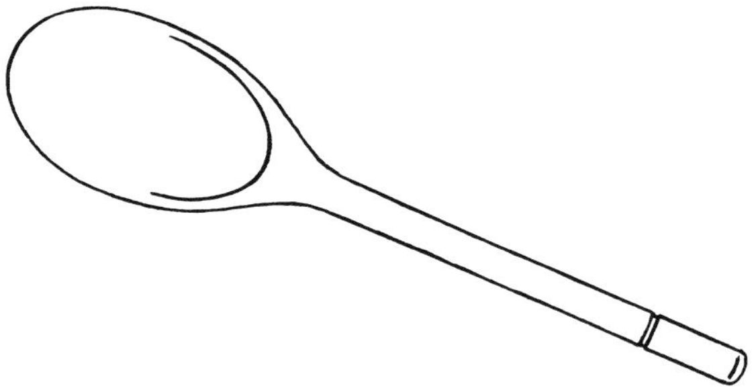

Say the word. Listen for the long /oo/ sound.

zoo moon food roof too

pool roof tooth spoon

tools cuckoo balloon

Blend to read the words.

oo oo

Say the sound. Trace the letters. Write the letters.

Say the words. Can you hear the long /oo/ sound?

Draw something with the long /oo/ sound (**oo**) in it.

Say the sounds

ai ee -igh oa -oo **oo**

**Name** ..................................................................... **Date** ..........................................................

ar

Say the sound. Trace the letters.

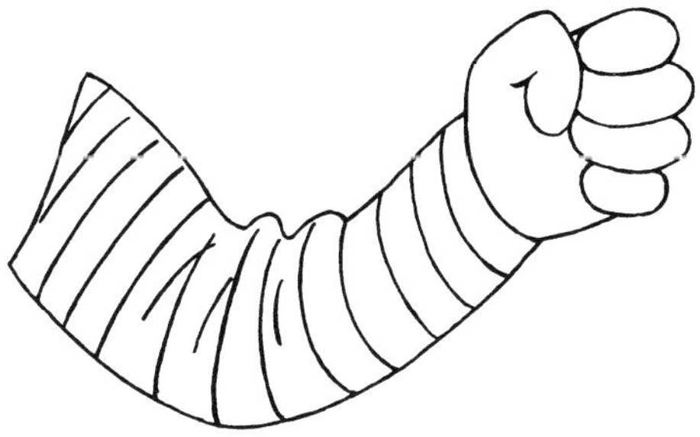

Say the word. Listen for the /ar/ sound.

art car farm park far

hard chart shark star

start garden market apart

Blend to read the words.

ar ar

Say the sound. Trace the letters. Write the letters.

Say the words. Can you hear the /ar/ sound?

Draw something with the /ar/ sound (**ar**) in it.

ee -igh oa -oo oo **ar**

**Name** ..............................................................  **Date** ..............................................................

# or

Say the sound. Trace the letters.

Say the word. Listen for the /or/ sound.

born fork torn for short

cork horn corn worn

shorts sport storm morning

Blend to read the words.

or or

Say the sound. Trace the letters. Write the letters.

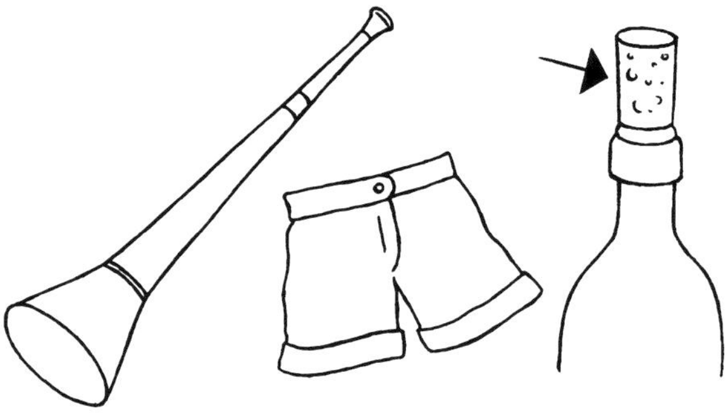

Say the words. Can you hear the /or/ sound?

Draw something with the /or/ sound (**or**) in it.

Say the sounds

ee -igh oa -oo oo ar **or**

**Name** ..............................................................

**Date** ..............................................................

ur

Say the sound. Trace the letters.

Say the word. Listen for the /ur/ sound.

fur turn hurt fur turn hurt

curls burn churn burnt

turnip burst slurp church

Blend to read the words.

ur ur

Say the sound. Trace the letters. Write the letters.

Say the words. Can you hear the /ur/ sound?

Draw something with the /ur/ sound (**ur**) in it.

Say the sounds

-igh oa -oo oo ar or **ur**

**Name** ..................................................................... **Date** ..........................................................

**ow**

Say the sound. Trace the letters.

Say the word. Listen for the /ou/ sound.

cow how now down owl

row bow town brown

frown clown crown crowds

Blend to read the words.

**ow** ow

Say the sound. Trace the letters. Write the letters.

Say the words. Can you hear the /ou/ sound?

Draw something with the /ou/ sound (**ow**) in it.

Say the sounds

oa -oo oo ar or ur **ow**

**Name** ..........................................................................  **Date** ..........................................................

oi

Say the sound. Trace the letters.

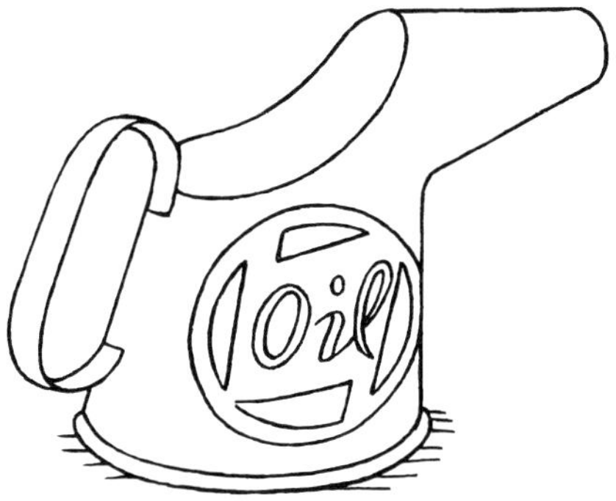


Say the word. Listen for the /oi/ sound.

foil coin soil oil foil boil

join coins point toilet

joint avoid spoil ointment

Blend to read the words.

oi oi

Say the sound. Trace the letters. Write the letters.

Say the words. Can you hear the /oi/ sound?

Draw something with the /oi/ sound (**oi**) in it.

Say the sounds

-oo oo ar or ur ow **oi**

**Name** ..............................................................  **Date** ..............................................................

# ear

Say the sound. Trace the letters.

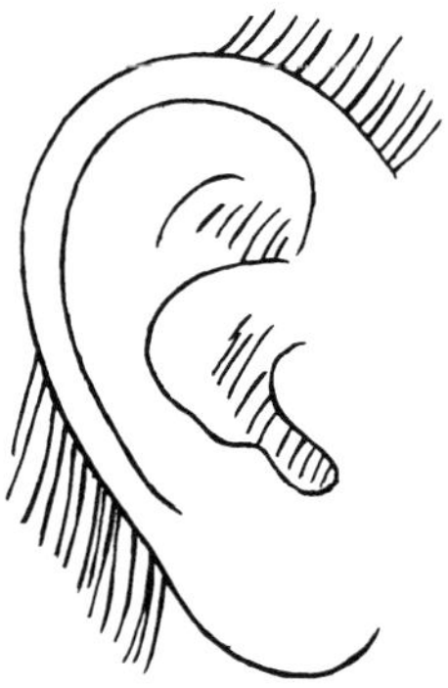

Say the word. Listen for the /eer/ sound.

ear hear fear ears tears

dear year gears shears

earring clear appear beard

Blend to read the words.

ear ear

Say the sound. Trace the letters. Write the letters.

Say the words. Can you hear the /eer/ sound?

Draw something with the /eer/ sound (**ear**) in it.

Say the sounds

oo ar or ur ow oi **ear**

**Name** ........................................................................ **Date** ..............................................................

# air

Say the sound. Trace the letters.

Say the word. Listen for the /air/ sound.

hair fair air lair fair hair

pair chair stairs pairs

upstairs downstairs chairman

Blend to read the words.

air air

Say the sound. Trace the letters. Write the letters.

Say the words. Can you hear the /air/ sound?

Draw something with the /air/ sound (**air**) in it.

ar or ur ow oi ear **air**

**Name** ..................................................................... **Date** ......................................................

**er**

Say the sound. Trace the letters.

Say the word. Listen for the /u/ sound.

sister boxer bother ladder

summer letter dinner

supper hammer winter

Blend to read the words.

**er** **er**

Say the sound. Trace the letters. Write the letters.

Say the words. Can you hear the /u/ sound?

Draw something with the /u/ sound (**er**) in it.

Say the sounds

or ur ow oi ear air **-er**

**Name** ..................................................................... **Date** ....................................................................

# er

Say the sound. Trace the letters.

Say the word. Listen for the /ur/ sound.

her fern kerb herd herbs

term verb stern hermit

perfect herbal mermaid

Blend to read the words.

er er

Say the sound. Trace the letters. Write the letters.

Say the words. Can you hear the /ur/ sound?

Draw something with the /ur/ sound (**er**) in it.

ur ow oi ear air -er **er**

**Name** ..................................................................... **Date** ........................................................

# ue

Say the sound. Trace the letters.

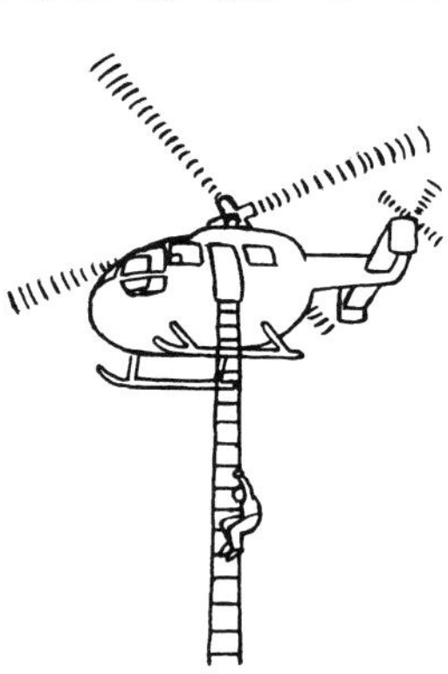

Say the word. Listen for the /yoo/ sound in it.

due cue value fuel venue

statue rescue argue

overdue barbecue queue

Blend to read the words.

ue ue

Say the sound. Trace the letters. Write the letters.

Say the words. Can you hear the /yoo/ sound?

Draw something with the /yoo/ sound (**ue**) in it.

Say the sounds

ow oi ear air -er er **-ue**

**Name** ..........................................................................  **Date** ..........................................................................

# ue

Say the sound. Trace the letters.

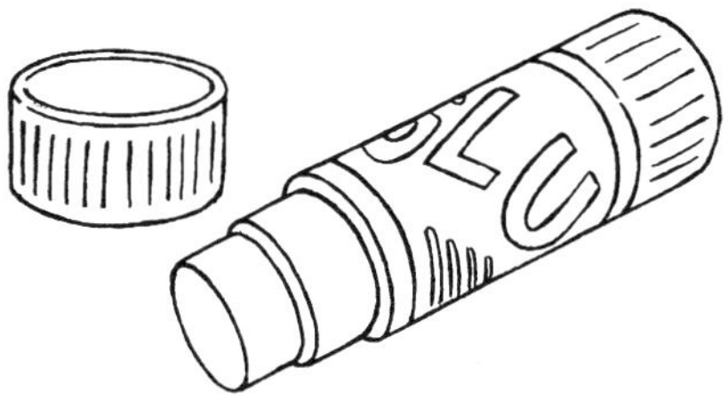

Say the word. Listen for the long /oo/ sound.

clue Sue true clue Sue

blue glue issue blue tissue

clueless tissues gruesome

Blend to read the words.

ue ue

Say the sound. Trace the letters. Write the letters.

Say the words. Can you hear the long /oo/ sound?

Draw something with the long /oo/ sound (**ue**) in it.

oi ear air -er er -ue **-ue**

**Name** ..........................................................  **Date** ..........................................................

ure    ture

Say the sound /yoor/. Trace the letters.

Say the sound /chu/. Trace the letters.

pure   cure

cured   secure

manure   manicure

Blend to read the words.

mixture   future

picture   vulture

adventure   lecture

Blend to read the words.

ure   ture

Say the sound. Trace the letters. Write the letters.

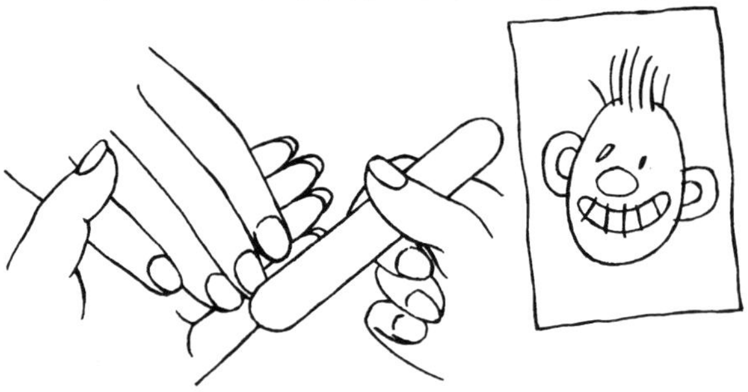

Say the words. Can you hear the /yoor/ and /chu/ sounds?

Draw something with the /yoor/ (**ure**) or /chu/ (**ture**) sounds in it.

ear  air  -er  er  **-ure**  **-ture**